MW00582322

# Divine Chuckles

## Life from a Higher Perspective

## Lin David Martin

numinous ♥ publishing

**numinous ♥ publishing**
Lin David Martin & Torill Elen Roennekleiv
PO Box 2063
Sedona, AZ 86339-2063
(1) 928-634-0803
numinous_publishing@yahoo.com
www.numinous-publishing.com

Copyright © 2005 by Lin David Martin
Cover art by Lin David Martin
Cover graphics by Mike Jung


All rights reserved.
This book, or parts of it,
may not be reproduced in any form
without permission,
except short excerpts
for review purposes.

ISBN: 0-9764352-0-9
Price in the USA - $18.95


Printed in the USA by
Lightning Source Inc.

# Content

# Foreword by Kevin Ryerson

Over the years, many people have told me about their excitement upon reading Shirley MacLaine's "Out On A Limb". And how this has opened up a spiritual path they could understand and follow.

A growing number of people of today are exploring various spiritual paths. Applied intuition, channeling, and the psychic sciences are carving deep inroads into the direction in which we, as a society, are moving. One major social impact of this is the extent to which meditation and self-hypnotic techniques are now acknowledged as valuable in restoring mental and physical well being. These techniques are widely applied in the areas of medicine, business and education. The works of people, such as Dr. Dean Ornish M.D., Ayman Fawaf (authored Exective E.Q.), Deepak Chopra M.D., and Dr. Gabriel Cousens M.D., to name just a few.

These same forces have had a profound impact in the area of nutrition. A few years ago, if we walked into our neighborhood grocery store and asked for a loaf of sprouted wheat bread or tofu, we would have been directed to the nearest health food store. Now, most of the major food chains have at least a small section of organic and unprocessed foods. Let alone the tremendous growth of produce retail channels – such as Whole Foods and Wild Oats. Many social scientists now accept that the holistic food and organic food movement can be traced back directly to the influential channeling of Edgar Cayce.

There has been significant impact on orthodox medicine as well, particularly in the application of biofeedback and visualization techniques in the treatment of a wide range of diseases, including hypertension, heart disease and cancer. More and more we are seeing empirical, scientific evidence of how the mind (or consciousness) and the body influence each other.

1

For anyone, like myself, who has long been a student of the works of channels such as Edgar Cayce and Jane Roberts, you will find the content of Lin David Martin's book *Divine Chuckles - Life from a Higher Perspective* to be a real treat. Unlike many other channeled works on the market, the material in this book comes almost exclusively and directly from the channeled source itself. The reader will find here carefully edited key transcripts, which allow the spiritual student to learn directly from an intuitive source.

In any study of the intuitive sciences, the highest application of any psychic ability is to discover ourselves in our relationship with God. That is the true goal of working with these energies. The highest application of any theory or model is in teaching us more about ourselves as beings of energy, and empowering us to achieve our fullest potential. This is what I feel *Divine Chuckles* helps us to attain. I am particularly enthusiastic about the psychic content of the final chapter "Timeless Thoughts for the Modern Mind."

Lin David Martin's career in the intuitive field has been long and distinguished. His peers and students have for some time encouraged him to compile a book of his powerful and profound teachings and readings. I think that readers of such works as Jess Stern's *The Sleeping Prophet*, *Oversoul 7* from Jane Roberts, and *Conversation with God* by Neale Donald Walsch, will find that *Divine Chuckles* will fit neatly into their spiritual library, as it does in my own. It is a gem of spiritual literature.

*Divine Chuckles - Life From A Higher Perspective* is unique in that indeed it is a workbook that can be assimilated at the reader's own pace. I think, however, that it will whet your appetite to such a degree that you will want to sit down over several evenings, or even in a single evening, to read and re-read this lucid spiritual literary piece. (www.kevinryerson.com)

# Introduction and Dedication

*Divine Chuckles - Life from a Higher Perspective*, has existed in manuscript form for many years. We are happy to finally get the book out into the public eye. The major part of *Divine Chuckles* is drawn from trance sessions done with various groups in USA, Denmark, Norway, Sweden and Germany in the years 1987–1988. The last two chapters are from trance classes in USA in the fall of 2004.

The trance material is timeless. It touches the truth that resides inside all of us, despite our different cultural backgrounds. I have felt honored to be a channel for Spirit over these many years. Of course I am still very human in the sense that we all experience an often painful awareness of our personal limitations.

I feel that this range of consciousness and compassion that Spirit brings, slowly opens more awareness and love for myself and others. I am blessed. Still a long way from where I would like to be, though I see the Light at the end of our collective tunnel.

There are so *very many* people who have made *Divine Chuckles* possible. To those who have made the obvious contributions in terms of time, energy and monetary support; my thanks with an overflowing heart go out to you. (You know who you are.)
Then on a deeper level, thank you all for the contributions that you shared in the different trance processes. You have by your presence helped to bring about a focus for Spirit to be of service in.

I know we as a human race are starting to wake up. It is to that collective sense of "Divine Hunger" coming forth in us all, that I with gratitude dedicate this book.

Peace and "Divine Chuckles" to us all.
*Lin David Martin - November 2004*

Chapter 1

# Recognizing The Presence Of Spirit

*It is our joy that we might share with you.*

*You have involved yourself*
*in the discovery of your consciousness,*
*and you would deepen to more understanding,*
*so the desire is fanned into a flame.*

*The sparks catch hold in your mind and deepen.*
*Out of that desire comes truth,*
*for it is in the essence of your search*
*that you need to look,*
*and determine what you want.*

*As you become more conscious*
*that you do desire that inner awakening,*
*bring to yourself the gift of the Spirit*
*to share with your fellow beings.*

*It may be very subtle or quite obvious,*
*but it is in the nature of consciousness,*
*the nature of your own awareness,*
*to become more complete.*

*As you begin to sense*
*that there is not just one dimension of reality,*
*but that reality speaks through many dimensions*
*and that you are a multi-dimensional being,*
*you begin to sense more of the truth*
*that encompasses you.*

Jesus said long ago, "In my Father's house are many mansions." You might reflect that he also said, "The Father and I are one; you and I are one," and, "The Kingdom of Heaven lies within you." Within you lie many mansions, many levels of awakening. As you cease to look upon yourself as limited to only the physical kingdom, you begin to sense the way of the Spirit in its gentleness and its compassion. It shall not force you, it shall not demand. It shall allow you your own search, your own seeking, your own desire. What is the path you would map out before you? Where would you go on the path of life?

You can move into heaven or hell - it is all the same in its essence, for there is neither in the ultimate sense. There is only Divinity. Term it what you will, but Divinity resides inherent in every cell in your body and every aspect of your consciousness. In all that you see surrounding you, Divinity is present.

The outer mind makes judgments; stepping over those things it considers problems, wanting to go carefully on life's path to find the easy way. Sometimes you might stub your toe on some of those rocks you thought were obstacles and find that it hurts a bit. But you find that you can step on the rock and gain a broader vision - with your increased height you can see further.

You may find others on the path too. It is much more fun to travel together for a time. Though you may ultimately go in different directions, all paths lead to the essence of Divine mind. So feel a bit of freedom and flexibility to explore, and yet most of all, to inherently follow your inner counsel - desiring it and following it, following it and desiring it - the two go together.

If at times you find you gather to you the impact of the Spirit and you do not always follow the guidance that comes, that too can be a learning process. For you will find that when you do not follow the guidance, things do not work as well.

6

When you do, things work very well and life becomes more joyous, more in the play of the child, more in the awakening of your deeper Self. Obstacles begin to dissolve, fears begin to drop, concerns and considerations of what others will think are no longer your primary perspective. You begin to sense that everybody wants the same energy consciousness, though they may not know it.

Why waste your time on the surface of life when you can dive deeply, partaking of Divinity through your meditations, your prayers, your times of coming together with others? In that partaking you recognize how beautiful they are. And in reflection, perhaps how beautiful you are as well.

It is not a mistake you have gathered together with those in your life. You have come together in a common purpose and vibration. As you gather many times over with those you know, and those you are yet to meet, and perhaps even recognize those present who are unseen and yet very present in their reality, it builds and strengthens the quickening of your consciousness. It builds a greater harmony of foundation upon which to rest the heavy burdens of life that you think you carry. You can let go of some of that. You do not have to carry around fears, guilts, doubts and such. Begin to sense how easy it is to stay in harmony if you listen quietly within and move with the impact of what your heart would have you do.

Grounding is also very important, primarily because for many of you the body does not get enough exercise. The oxygen, the movement of the body, the strengthening of your muscles creates an easy opening for consciousness, a working vehicle where energy may be present in its radiance and you feel good about yourself. That helps.

Give yourself the blessing of talking with others about their inner process, perhaps sharing dreams or a time of meditation.

7

Perhaps a little energy work with another. Perhaps a little yoga.

Those things need not take a long time. You can find in so doing that your body quickens, your consciousness quickens and life becomes truly exciting in the Divine sense of purpose being recognized and revealed. And remember to hold the child within you as part of your beauty.

It may sound rather complex, but these processes are essentially built upon the desire to feel the joy and the love of the Spirit and to know yourself. For the Divinity you are is of great joy. It is easy to get caught up in the world and the events around you in the physical dimension, but if you place the greatest importance on your inner world and place relative importance on your external world, you will find truth becoming a natural part of your awakening.

Be joyous. Be not long-faced, even if you hit difficulties in your process. Be happy that you hit them, so you can help them to dissolve. Be prepared to meet many others moving through a similar process, happy to share the burdens all have seemingly accepted as real. Distribute the weight a bit so the burden is less. And finally perhaps, allow its dissolvement so it is non-existent.

Be prepared to meet those you might call mates on a Soul level, not those you romantically call your soul-mate, but those who have a similar vibration. Have great joy at the recognition of the beauty of others. Consider the simplicity of life and the great complexity of life both being present. As the mind quiets, the Spirit moves stronger and your Divinity may become quite apparent to you.

Be prepared to accept a bit of personal responsibility for how you act and think. But most of all, accept out of your joy of self-discovery a sense of inter-linked energy with the Spirit, helping you to understand yourself even more deeply, more quickly.

As you do that you may find a lot of energy flowing through you to help others in their need.

You become something of a channel or a vehicle in a way the outer mind can understand. You are always doing that anyway, but it is nice when you can understand it and move with it in a harmonious way. Be prepared to be Divine. Nothing else will do. Pat yourself on the back occasionally and say, "You are looking pretty good! I like the Divinity I see in you." And do the same for others.

Doing this will help you stop the game the outer mind has of not knowing that it knows. Then you will be in good shape. You will have a lot of friends in the Spirit whom you will come to understand you have always known. Think about it. It is an act of free choice. To move more deeply into heavenly states, to move more deeply into the knowingness of the body as a vehicle, is quite beautiful.

Perhaps there are those areas now that may be as questioning in your thinking. We would be happy to expose you to your own knowing if you want.

*I have heard about the extinction of individuality on the Soul level. Does the soul retain individuality all the time?*

What do *you* want?

*I tend to feel that I want individuality.*

You can have it! [laughter] You do not ever lose individuality. It is just a matter of where you want to place the focus. When you have reached a state of great enlightenment, you can focus on the small element of personality remaining - like the drop in the ocean. Or you can focus on the ocean. The drop has the ocean - the individual has universal mind. Or you can say the ocean has the drop. Both are true.

9

Everybody wants to retain their ego. What for? You can retain your individuality. The ego is doing the job now that it needs to do, but in time it will become unimportant. You will still retain your uniqueness. That is the gift of the Divine. You will not lose that. I think that pertains to your question in its deeper sense.

*Could you give me information on releasing anger toward someone?*

Well, I think everybody knows what you mean. Not in the intimacy of detail, but in the basic process of trying to live life without holding anger and resentment toward others - trying to awaken yourself without feeling you still dislike someone. If you feel there is need of forgiveness, then by all means go ahead and forgive as best you can. But on a deeper level I want you to understand that the only forgiveness that needs to be extended, is forgiveness of self.

Divine mind in its perfection will give everyone the opportunity to meet their actions - sometimes they are called karmic - so that they may evolve out of states of consciousness where negativity might exist and begin to build a deeper understanding of how love works.

Ultimately karma is dissolved, as you think of negative karma, and only the positive karma remains: the gifts of insight, wisdom and joy that you give yourself. Ultimately, in forgiving others you are only forgiving self of self's limitations. Divine mind in its perfection has already forgiven them and if you hold anger, it is just a little hook that holds you back until you *let go and let God*, so to speak. Just think of the healing of past patterns as a bolstering of ego confidence so that you can grow more quickly.

*My mind is very alert and active when my body is a total wreck. The moment I move my body, my mind gets tired.*

10

Are you doing any exercise?

*Not much. When I do exercise my mind gets tired.*

Well, I think you will find a point where that stops happening and your mind is at rest either way. Not tired, but actively awake either way. Get more oxygen in the body, do some things you like to do that are rather physically strenuous, not hard in the sense of being forced, but joyfully done.

*I have found that if I do a lot of physical exercise, my mind stands still.*

Maybe that's a good place for it to be. Did you ever think about that? [laughter]

*Yes, but I am much happier when I am in my mind. I feel so very limited when I am just in my body.*

The integration of body, mind and Spirit very much calls forth heaven. When you are in your mind you are unable to make physical expression. If you have no physical expression, is there not something missing?
You are eating sugars? Coffees and teas and chocolates and such?

*Yes.*

You have low blood sugar. Get rid of the stimulants, exercise the body for about a month, then come back and see me! [laughter] I think you will tell me how the body and mind can work in tandem, like two horses pulling together, beautifully. You have to try it. You'll like it!

No coffees, no teas, no stimulants and no sugar in refined form. A little bit of fruit is okay. Get the body happy through exercise in a way you enjoy and you will have a very fine time doing what you want to do - moving through the energies of your own choice without feeling this dilemma you speak of.

11

You cannot understand this until you try it. So I suggest you try it. Okay? It is the only way you are going to prove me wrong. You might prove yourself right, in the real sense.

*Is there a certain way to go into trance?*

No, there is not. Love. Love of the Spirit. Love of others. Love of self. Being around it, perhaps, would be the most active way of getting in touch with the energy. But do not overlook the amount of love that can flow in any form of healing activity. Then you begin to see that trance is just a matter of shifting levels of consciousness. When you get comfortable with the shifting processes you can employ, you begin to see it as part of the same overall process. It is a bit of a specialty, that's all.

*How can I get to know my teachers?*

By wanting to. Once a week, have a special meditation: asking them to give you an idea of how they work with you. What they do in your life. What their name is - their vibration. And then the rest of the week just meditate on the various things of life, such as love and patience and the trees and the water and healing. In the special meditation once a week, ask of your teachers their knowledge and their presence. It will happen rather quickly.

*Can you always trust your inner voice?*

You can always trust the deep inner levels of your inner voice. Whether you can trust the monkey mind, which may masquerade a bit, is another question.

*How can I come to grips with what you call my "monkey mind?"*

Make friends with it. Just say, "Hi monkey, I like you." Sometimes you know you're a monkey, though! Make friends. Don't make enemies. The monkey is important. But see it as just a monkey. Then you will have a good friend - a good monkey friend.

*I have a hard time seeing it as the monkey.*

Well, how do you want to see it? As a zebra? [laughter]
The main thing is just to recognize that the outer mind always wants to create separation. It will tell you that you are missing the boat, that you are doing it wrong, and on and on. If you sense that it has that built-in predisposition toward limitation, then you can befriend it at the level of its own capacity to serve, without feeling like it should have its own way all the time.

Recognize your own Divinity. Be proud of yourself and recognize what is going on in the deeper sense of your Spiritual awakening. When you do that, you see more of the totality. The full functioning, the full flowering of that Divine Self within you, will provide resources and answers to much that you now think is problematic. You will begin to see these problems as stepping-stones along the way. Be proud of yourself.

We shall go now. It has been our great joy to share with you.

Good evening. God bless you.

13

# Meditation

*Recognize the possibility
of feeling the presence of the Spirit.*

*Begin to open your heart
to the sense of love you desire to experience,
and invite those who work with you as teachers
to be present.*

*Begin to acknowledge your own Divinity
by sensing the Divinity in others.*

*If there is someone you feel concerned about,
mentally place them in some beautiful part of nature.
Ask their higher Self to draw in energy,
using that energy in any way that is appropriate.*

*Ask that you might be used as a channel;
That the Universe may flow energy
through you to this person,
and that their higher Self may receive the energy.
Let a deep sense of love, of light, move to them.*

*Allow that they have received energy
in the way most appropriate for them.*

*Acknowledge your own Divinity
by sensing the Divinity in all things.*

*Contemplate and feel the energy
of the planet and nature at its most beautiful.
Sense the rocks, the trees, the ocean, the mountains.*

*Very gently, envision yourself*
*in beautiful, natural surroundings.*
*Feel the radiance of the sun.*
*Feel the beauty of the wind.*
*Feel yourself deeply*
*in resonance and communion with the earth.*

*Ask that you might be more aware*
*of the counsel of the Spirit.*
*Ask to feel personal contact with a Spiritual teacher,*
*that your heart may be more permanently opened,*
*and the shape of your perception fulfilled in wholeness.*

*Gently allow yourself to receive a deep sense of love.*

*Give thanks for the presence of the Spirit,*
*and the energy you have experienced.*

*May your attitude toward life be such*
*that you receive the sense of the joy*
*that underlies all experience.*

Chapter 2

# Awakening To The Divinity Within

*God bless you.*
*It is our joy that we might share with you,*
*for you have been finding in your own way*
*a deeper richness of the Spirit.*
*Coming to focus on those things your heart holds dear,*
*you look within to find answers.*
*You look within self to reveal that deeper contact with the Spirit.*
*And it is forthcoming.*

*As you move into your heart with devotion,*
*that aspect of devotion becomes your greater process.*
*As you move to the depths of your own being*
*you find there the witness of the Spirit.*
*You find the holiness you seek "somewhere" in the universe,*
*dwelling even within you.*
*Discovering that through the desire of the heart,*
*more of the larger heart of the Universe comes to you.*

*Be privileged to meet that which you desire,*
*for in the deep part of your heart,*
*as you welcome the Divine in,*
*the Divine takes residence and begins*
*the gentle art of transformation.*

*Transformation need never be forced.*
*You may have the thought that you have to do something*
*to receive the beauty of the Spirit,*
*yet always that beauty surrounds you.*
*You do not have to do something*
*in order to be worthy to receive it.*
*Simply stand aside with the conscious mind,*

*setting aside its opinions, thoughts, judgments and doubts, and allow self to open to the deeper mind.*

Many people around the world have given everything they could to touch the deeper mind. They have sought in high places. They have dug into the depths of caves and such. They have figuratively traversed great distances of mind in order to find the Spirit. And yet it is so simple. A small child may easily evoke that presence. In their attitude of honesty, wonderment and joy, it comes forth. In the observation of life through the eyes of the child, often there is deep wisdom. You have had that before, each of you. It has been present. And it comes again, that you might witness the child-mind that touches the deeper dimension of Self.

You do not have to give all of your consciousness to one point in time. This will be a continuing process. It need not be thought that now you have the ultimate answer and can rest assured nothing more is needed. If the ultimate answer could be given in words, mankind would have been awakened long ago. Words are tools to point the direction in which your consciousness may flow, allowing the evocation of your own Divinity, finding the deepest response of yourself to the Divine in all things. That is far beyond the measure of words to induce.

Words are gentle reminders. They are not the energy of truth itself. The truth shall not be that which you find written in a book or spoken in verbal form. It is that which awakens your inner being to the awareness that the truth of life is present now, has been, and shall always be present, even within yourself, even within all things around you. And therefore there is no great effort needed on your part to make God happen. God is happening. You need not say to your neighbor, "Know God, because you should, and it is right, and it will make you happy." That is a worthy admonition - a worthy viewpoint - but if you know God, you do not have to say to another, "Know God."

19

You simply are your own being and the energy you express witnesses to them their own beauty, that they might awaken to the Divine more quickly.

Nothing against words, mind you. They are vehicles of consciousness. But everyone thinks the word's proper sequencing must be found in order to evoke some ancient form of magic to bring forth truth, in order that it may strike another like a blow and say to them, "You must believe thusly." Truth does not say you must believe thusly. It is in a re-awakening, a reassurance of how Divine each one is. The words come later, in trying to approximate that awareness.

Move past the words of your conviction; the views of your heart expressed in pantomime as though you were dancing before the light and looking at the shadow on the wall, saying, "There is truth. The shadow is truth." The words are the absence of truth with which you paint the picture, hoping to allude to its greater reality. Let go of the words and dive deeply into your Soul consciousness.

Transformation comes gently. You shall never find God making you do something. Always it will be by your own choice to work in harmony with what you come to know. The knowingness will be deep and yet the outer mind can still have doubt. The knowingness will be present just the same. The more you feel correspondence in outer thought, outer action, with the inner desire, the inner truth that lies within you, then shall you find happiness. But if you find not happiness, it is because *you* have not allowed it to flow. For it is not so much the circumstances that surround you in your outer life that creates or allow happiness - it is your own perception, your own attitude, your own ability to see deeply. And if you have deep seeing, then you see God. If not, then you see only man in the narrowness of that concept. You do not see the deeper part of mankind.

Let your own wisdom come. It may overshadow you gently, or at times be quite strong, but it will come as you desire. No one can place it there for you. No one can make wisdom happen. Only you hold the key to your own greater advancement.

Your teachers will work closely with your ability to receive, but they will not force you to receive anything for which you are not ready. They honor your growth. They do not desire to make for you the quick and easy path if it does not serve your growth. They will always honor your growth. They will not fail you in that sense. They may fail you in the sense that your outer mind thinks, "Why don't my teachers come and tell me this? Why didn't they help me avoid that mistake?" Those concepts may arise in the outer mind, but inwardly you know the truth: that you have been at the point of choice. You have made decisions to walk the path of your own choosing. No one has made it for you. Your teachers will help you, but they will not change your life unless you will that they might help. Then they can do that.

Again, it is not so much a matter of tuning into teachers as such. It is a matter of going to the depth of your own being. And they will honor your vibrational pattern by sharing with you the same vibration they carry. So it is a joint process always, in a very deep way.

You have perhaps wondered what it would be like to be a trance channel, or a powerful healer: One who can see the future, or one who in clairvoyance might see the aura, reading thoughts and patterns of life process. Such is worthy consideration, but think about who you really are; your own truth - your own deep nature. Do not get caught in thinking, "When will I be psychic? When will I be famous? When will I be able to heal other people dramatically?" Have more awareness of, "I work with my own process. I go deep. I follow my own thoughts and I look to see where the thoughts may be balanced and where they may be out of balance,

21

and I work to bring those balance points in."

That would be a proper level of manifestation for each of you. And out of that will come gifts from the Spirit.

That can be quite dramatic. It can be a lot of fun and very exciting. But it does not change the basic person. It allows a more perceptive process. And you will see yourself more clearly. But it does not create change. It does not force change. Only you can allow change. No one can force you.

Think then of the simplicity of your own allowance. What will you allow yourself to receive? What joy will you allow to come into your life? What structure do you rigidly hang on to? Are you hanging on to structures of the past? Are you hanging on to thoughts that you would like to somehow move into another sense of self? There may be things you have thought about yourself that you want to share. Share those things as you can. Share those things which are of value, to understand yourself more completely.

The more you work with the patterns of your own awareness, the more you will see how Divine you are in your essence. You will also know how far it seems you are from that Divinity in your day-to-day existence. What to do about such separation might be a worthy question. The true heart knows no separation. The outer mind in analysis knows nothing but separation.

You will find as you move through life that separation breeds falsehood and does not give truth. You will become more conscious of the truth residing within each person, not at the mercy of some stern God in the heavens. Within each person lies the full flowering of the Universe - the full power of creation. In each heart, each person has truth magnificently present. You will move closer to that.

Gently approach the throne of the Divine in your meditations and prayer. Let your daily thoughts reflect that greater reality. Know that the attitude in which you hold life is the attitude which will be reflected to you. If you think life is terrible, so it shall be until you purify your attitude and recognize the power of your own vehicle of consciousness. If you think life is an open door to the Universe, then you have assessed it correctly. It is that.

Ask the presence of your awakening to come. Ask that the hand of the Divine shall be in your life in all things. Ask that you might have deeper trust. Ask that you might be clear. The awakening you share with others will also be one which you taste. So that it is not from memory: "Oh, I remember when I was awakened, and it felt thusly." It is an aspect of the present state. You can say, "It happened thusly," and be correct, but how is it happening? Is it happening thusly now? That is the question. Not that you need more questions. You have too many as it is! But hold the thought of, "Where does Divinity dwell?" It dwells in the heart of each one. And largely are those peoples unconscious of it so in-dwelling. Just the same, it is there. If you look and you have the eyes of the Spirit to witness truth within another, it speaks to you beyond words.

Joy is at the heart of all things. Even that which appears to be sadness or turmoil, at its heart, is joy. The joy overcomes that which seems as separation. It does not bring division into smaller pieces - it brings unity.
Gently now, trust yourselves. That is the answer you seek. What more could we say to you in words, we wonder? But I am confident your outer mind will have that which you term as questioning.

*I would like to know more about how to integrate my ego.*

Love it. More love. Then you will see its beauty, its true presence. You will see it as a gift. Not as something to take joy away. But something to create the difference of consciousness, that allows you the sense of separation, so you can then have the sense of re-connection. And in re-connection you find joy.

*How I can get a sense of strength, and own my own power?*

Stop using stimulants in the body. They rob the body of a feeling of power. The body and self, as you emotionally experience yourself, are closely linked. It is hard for people to hear that, but strength of the physical body will strengthen your sense of self as well. The body is the vehicle. The body is the channel. There is no limit to the energy of heaven, but the body has a limit to what it can handle. When the body is strengthened, you find yourself more powerful in the deeper sense. Not strengthening of muscles, but strengthening of your sense of physical resonance with the planet - physical wholeness. With that will come a sense of your emotional, mental, and Spiritual wholeness as well. And do not worry about it. It is not a problem. Enjoy the opening that comes, as the body gets stronger.

*Sometimes I am open, and very much in my heart in gentleness and love, yet it doesn't feel like a strength.*

That is only the ego's perception of strength. As the love grows stronger you will see that the old idea of strength is limited. Gentleness is its own strength. It will become clearer for you how that energy works. With love, much happens. Without love, everything becomes difficult. It is not the strength to overcome the difficulty the personality would exercise, if no love were there. It is the strength to find no difficulty because love *is* there.

24

*Could you give me some advice for my meditation?*

Do a visualization of the heart chakra. It is very simple. Also, connect with the earth. It does not have to be complicated to work. It would be good to get grounded first, then you can meditate easily.

*Is feeling vulnerable a natural process of opening up?*

Oh, of course. To feel a bit more vulnerable is also to begin to ask your guidance to show you that you are not alone, else most people would not ask. It helps to loosen the ego's own desire and will, which says, "I know what is best for me." Vulnerability assists in reaching a point where the ego mind loosens, and says, "Perhaps I don't know everything that is best for me. Perhaps I should better ask for some guidance, some help, some counsel." Then the ego feels vulnerable - when the heart grows stronger. In actuality, vulnerability in that sense becomes strength. If you see that feeling come, it is okay. Just work a little with the grounding to go along with the opening.

I think it is good we do not hold the body longer. Let there be in the thought structure of each of you, the consciousness that you know, in an ultimate sense, you are Divine, and now you are just waking up to it. Let the waking up process be gentle, stretching here and there, letting yourself wake up gently. As you awaken you will notice the presence of those you have called teachers. You will notice the presence of energy in others which leads to the door of their own consciousness, so that you can communicate - you can share, you can find the God in others. And in that way, know the God that resides within you, equally present. Either way, diving deep within Self or looking in the heart of others, you will find Divinity present.

We will close now. It has been our great joy to share with you.

Good evening. God bless you.

# Meditation

*Allow a sense of light to fill your body.*
*Feel light flowing up from the earth,*
*through your feet and legs,*
*flooding your body,*
*moving into every cell.*

*Now begin to sense energy from the heavens,*
*radiantly flowing down into every cell of your body.*

*Very gently,*
*sense light flowing more intensely*
*into each of the chakras,*
*bringing a sense of balance,*
*of connection with the earth.*

*Focus on any center,*
*any chakra in the body*
*that feels low on energy.*
*Let more light,*
*more love flow into that area.*

*Allow a sense of transformation,*
*a sense of wholeness.*
*Feel the deep longing*
*for the Spirit you hold within,*
*drawing to you*
*an inner sense of guidance and awakening.*

*Sense,*
*visualize,*
*feel,*

*the light flowing in the body,*
*beautifully balanced.*

*Gradually, draw from your thoughts*
*any area that feels awkward.*
*It may be something in your personality.*
*It may be something in your relationships with others.*

*Draw that particular awkward energy out.*
*Place it in the very center of light*
*flowing between heaven and earth.*
*Gently let the light bring transformation and healing.*

*Allow the light to flow back into your body,*
*bringing that awkward area,*
*renewed,*
*balanced,*
*back as a strength.*

*Feel what might have been awkwardness*
*now as a growing awareness,*
*growing insight.*
*Bless yourself in the process.*

*Very gently now,*
*allow yourself to feel the light in the body*
*connecting with the earth,*
*bringing a deep sense*
*of peace and balance.*

Chapter 3

# Inner Change –
# The Gift Of Awakening Consciousness

*God bless you.*
*It is our joy that we might share with you.*

*In order that you may find your own way of consciousness,*
*it is important that you stop thinking*
*that the truth is out there somewhere,*
*far from you.*

*Begin to delve inside your consciousness*
*to the point where you*
*start to trust your own inner knowing.*
*For there are those ways,*
*both obvious and subtle,*
*in which consciousness may shift.*

*That which is most important*
*is the willingness to begin to trust.*
*The willingness to begin to*
*seek out truth that you may find it.*
*For if you trust what comes,*
*more will come.*
*And if you do not trust what comes,*
*then try to test it a bit.*
*See what may be there.*

*Do not just cast it aside as though it is not important,*

*as though it is a figment of your imagination.*
*Test it to see how it fits,*
*how it feels,*
*how it serves in your life.*

*If you give yourself that opportunity to grow,*
*then you will in a sense be asking for more.*
*And when you have eaten of that plate,*
*you have allowed yourself room*
*for more food of the Spirit to be served.*
*And so it will be.*

Now is a time of good change in the world. There is an inner change taking place. And that is why everyone feels life shifting so quickly. That is why you find so much divorce and re-marriage. Such rapid shifts in occupations. People changing curriculums in their schooling. People finding new ways to explore and then trying something else. There is a great variety and opportunity that surrounds you. And usually there is not much patience.

So it is that the outer mind often feels resistant and threatened by the inner change taking place. Or it may think it desires change. But often it seeks change for the sake of change, not for the sake of experience. Look a little deeper. Ask for an awareness from within to show you what is taking place.

It is actually quite a gradual process that the inner Self shoves you through, or allows you to flow through. In truth nobody pushes from within, though it may feel that way. If you were giving birth to a child, would you not have to push a bit? So it is that the inner Self governs your true awakening and gives birth in your consciousness to a new dimension. So there may feel to be a push. But what a marvelous time in which to live! What a wonderful time to be birthed!

It is a time when you can awaken in your consciousness. It is that sense of growing awareness that there is a change taking place that is rather beautiful - the awareness that the world is not suddenly going to fall apart. Everywhere it is happening. You may find trouble spots in the world where war and rumor of war exists, and wonder why that is so if there is such an awakening. What you find there is resistance to change. The fear of change. The outer mind getting caught in its religiosity and its idea of how God should be. And when that idea from within is being threatened, then the outer mind may resist all the more and create fanaticism. But that shall pass. It shall move aside.

Mankind shall begin in a few decades to truly live in brotherhood. The threat of war shall pass. The time of affiliation with one nation exclusively shall pass. You shall begin to see that you are planetary citizens. You are members of one planet, and that there are other planets too, that you will join with in friendship. Those present now that you call the UFO's are not foreign to you. They are in the same vibratory process of growth and evolution. They are perhaps a step or two ahead of you on the evolutionary ladder, but no different in their essence. In their desire to assist, you shall find that you are part of a great Universe, a great sea of consciousness. This is not just in the theoretical sense, but in the true sense of others that you relate to as individuals, who come to share their energy with you.

You are not on the planet alone. Many of you are conscious that you have guidance. And so shall that consciousness of guidance expand. You will begin to see that the planet is simultaneously present on many dimensions of life. You inhabit the physical body, but you also are part of the Spirit. This adds dimension to your consciousness.

It is a powerful process to be in the body now. You can grow out of the body too, but you have planned for very long to be in the body. You have put much energy into the preparation for this time. So be aware of what you have given yourselves: the gift of consciousness, the gift of awakening.

You will continue. As a personality there may come much change. As a Soul being, there will come the slow and evolutionary process of your awakening. Because as a personality, whether you believe it or not, you could not handle much more awakening. So let the outer mind slip within. Find the integration point. Find the nurturing. Allow yourself to feel the privilege of being on the planet. Let your change in attitude be real.

Let there be a sense that you come closer to a feeling of the essence of life, a feeling of awe, a feeling of respect and admiration for life itself.

Think about your own personal life and where it leads you. Think about the power of your mind to create. Watch carefully what you desire, for sometimes your desires are very accurate and on schedule for what you need, and other times your desires are passing fancies and may draw you aside into a little side current of life. That too, is all right. You can learn that way, but be clear with what you truly desire, that it may more quickly manifest. And it shall manifest. For as you desire, you attract to you that which you desire.

Look at the mind and how it functions. Look below the surface. See the different layers of consciousness you carry. Begin to investigate how it is that more love and more compassion may be part of your daily reality. Look into the adventure that healing and the opportunities for sharing your talent of psychic awareness may bring. Begin to see yourself as a bit of a channel for the Spirit.

Begin to see that the Universe is not limited through you or anyone else. Where blockage is, there may come salvation. Or as you call it: the salve of consciousness - the way of healing - to the mind and the Spirit. In that way you may move forward and cast aside your self-doubt, your self-pity, your self-fear. All of those things cause limitation. Step forward into a brighter day of your own creation!

That is coming. It shall come to pass in the outer levels of your consciousness. The limits of the outer mind may be bypassed or dissolved. So be not weak in your fear. Be strong in your ability to accept your own beauty. That is true strength. And that strength you shall share with others that they might see their beauty too. A true gift of love comes as you do that.

Perhaps we can now look at those areas, which may seem as questions for you.

*Does the use of drugs, such as marijuana, mushrooms and psychedelics, aid to awaken Spiritual consciousness - or damage it?*

For many, drugs are a point of experimentation until there is reasonable confidence through direct experience that: Yes, the mind is multi-dimensional. Yes, there are levels of consciousness, which are more perceptive. And yes, you do have Divinity within you. Please know that those elements of drugs do not give you Divinity. They give you a sense of its presence so that you might move forward, but then at some point they need to be released. They are tools for many that suddenly for some become blockage. For others they may continue to serve as tools for a time, but ultimately they will be set aside for a more direct perception of reality, unclouded by the chemical atmospheres that they bring.

*Is there physical damage when drugs are used?*

It depends on the chemical element of course, but for some whose bodies are quite sensitive, drugs could very easily be damaging. For others the body may be such that it is not so sensitive, and they will not feel much damage. It depends on the element. If you take a strong psychedelic drug, it may render an individual - with the chakras not capable of closing in the proper manner - permanently imbalanced. If you take strong mushrooms or peyote or a strong drug such as LSD, you may experience states of consciousness the personality cannot integrate. And it may leave a permanent residue of fear of overload, as though you had blown a fuse or two and are frightened you will do so again. It may cut away then, the desire and the integrity of your search.

For some it has opened the door. They have been rather closed in their attitude and suddenly they say, "Aha, more of truth is available. I will seek it." So it is not that you can make a blanket statement and say drugs are good or bad, but simply that they are stepping stones along the way on which some choose to walk. Others do not have the need to do so.

*There seems to be another side to consciousness. How does one make peace with the shadow side of self?*

First of all, I think it is helpful to think of that part of your mind as the monkey. By way of illustration; if you find fear coming and you know in very reasonable logical terms that there is no reason for fear, yet it comes, recognize it as the monkey playing the game of not knowing. Playing the game of feeling separate. Playing the game of saying, "I am alone in the universe. Nobody is with me." This is the game the monkey plays.

You look at that part of self. You do not get mad at it. You do not need to be mad at the self. Love that part of your being that feels fear. Pat it on the head a little bit and say, "You are going to grow up. Don't worry. We'll find more love coming for you so you won't have so much fear." In that sense you deepen your confidence to move with a little meditation and prayer, and work with those energy states that move you past the point of the monkey. You begin to sense your own deeper union with the Divine Source. In that way - whether through loving others and seeing their Divinity, or loving self - you will begin to make friends with the monkey. And in that way you allow integration.

It is easy to say, "Love thyself. Love thy Lord, thy God with all thy heart, mind and soul. And love thy neighbor." Most of you would agree that loving self is perhaps the most difficult. Loving thy neighbor is a good way to love thyself.

35

Certainly to love the Divinity is to find self in a deeper sense. So they all revolve around the center of consciousness that you might term the ability to allow love. That is the point of light in which those three points of view come into focus.

If nothing else works, and you feel the monkey mind going crazy, ask in the form of a prayer for more compassion for yourself. It is amazing how well it works. Everybody forgets to extend compassion to their own being. They are so quick to send a little healing to others. Ask for healing for self too.

*Occasionally one might experience peak moments of consciousness, but it seems so difficult to maintain when dealing with ordinary daily events. How do we move toward a more constantly awakened state?*

You will find that more will come. But it will be a gradual process. Subtly it begins to overshadow your consciousness, rather than dramatically. You simply wake up and begin to feel that you can be happy all the time, even when you are feeling miserable. That is a distinct advantage over just being miserable. [laughter]

It is a gradual integration process and it calls for a bit of patience. Not resignation, but expectation of the end results. Have the desire, the hope and the openness to allow it. Also look at some of the practical attitudes that must be dealt with on a day-to-day basis. How effective is your manifestation on the physical plane? What do you want to manifest? What do you want to connect to?

Nothing is bad in itself. So it is not to say that some things are bad for you and some things are good. It is more to say, "This I find in balance with my being, this I do not. I will let go of that. Perhaps others would like to do that, but I do not." That kind of attitude - which is a slow refinement - will allow more joy to come.

In the meantime, let your active search continue. Seek out the connections with other people that feel important. Look for the wisdom that may lie in the written word. Look for the attitudes of change that you may feel through exposure to music, or to a sense of your own inner song or mantra. It is kind of a constant or daily prayer state that you enter into, even if but for five minutes.

All of this begins to make the gradual process of change available to you. The outer mind will still feel resistant at the amount of time it may seem to take. But that time is relatively short and it is time that is important for your overall integration. So your teachers are quick to bring you joy often, but it is something that slowly integrates. You would find an imbalance if you suddenly felt joy all the time. So be patient and expectant at the same time. It will come.

# Meditation

*Gently let the energy build*
*in your feeling self.*

*Allow the light to flow in and through you*
*as a healing essence.*

*Let the sense of light,*
*of healing,*
*of love,*
*be present*
*in every cell of your body.*

*Wake up to love.*
*That is the next step for you*
*in this pattern of life.*

*There is great love for you*
*in the Spirit.*
*You are deeply loved.*

*Acknowledge more and more*
*that sense of love*
*over and above all else*
*that you feel or do,*
*say or think.*

*God bless you.*

# Chapter 4

# Integrating Guidance –
# Making Friends With The Higher Self

*God bless you.*

*It is a joy that we might share with you,*
*for each of you provides,*
*in your own way,*
*a door to an awakening consciousness.*

*As you learn to love yourself more deeply,*
*you push that door open ever wider.*
*When you feel lack of love for self and others,*
*you close the door just a bit.*

*The rise and fall of a given pattern*
*is like a swinging pendulum.*
*You may find your sense of self-awareness*
*expanding and then retreating,*
*but in actuality you are moving forward*
*even when you feel you are retreating.*
*For the cumulative effect of your overall process*
*is one of growth.*

That may be hard to see in certain instances, but it is nonetheless true. Many of you have awakened memories of other lives. You have a growing sense of the guidance of the Spirit that intermingles in your daily thoughts and a greater sense of the goal and gift of your inheritance - your heritage in this body that you carry. That gift is the power the body has as a vehicle in which expansion of consciousness may take place.

You find yourself standing on the threshold of what might be termed a new age of awareness. While that may be a rather provocative term, it nonetheless has an energy of truth about it. For mankind is ready now to make the final link to the deeper mind, which has been denied because you have not been ready. You are moving to the point of readiness to re-awaken the consciousness you have always carried. The sense of self - the sense of selfhood - has blocked this consciousness.

In your individualization, needs and process, you have not been ready to approach the deeper Self. But it comes - more and more it comes. It comes gently. It comes as it needs to come. Sometimes in ways you may find a bit mysterious, a bit paradoxical, but that awareness comes. It gently integrates and overwhelms your normal consciousness with its greater truth, its greater joy, its greater insight and awareness.

What you move into is what you might call the Golden Age. It will not mean that everybody sits around playing harps. You are not going to pave your streets with gold. You will find that the integration process takes you ever deeper into new layers of selfhood. To analyze, to contrast with the past, and to re-awaken more love so that you come to greater depths of power - which is the essence of love.

Love is not something weak with no effect. It is the singularly most powerful energy you shall encounter. The forms of love are many. There are various terms and meanings but the essence is the same. The essence is of deep compassion. It reaches out to touch others in their growth, while continuing to allow your evolution.

The deepest levels of compassion have no lack of insight for they see the Divinity in everyone. Those levels of compassion will move you in profound ways in touching your own growth, your own joy, your own creative energies to manifest those things which you might call miraculous, as well as those things which are more ordinary.

What is the miracle of consciousness itself that you carry? What is the miracle of having a body to function through? It is to have the time and space, as you know it, in order to grow. Is that less miraculous because it is familiar? As an illustration, there is ultimately nothing wrong with anyone. If you could see that and know it, would it appear to be a miracle if it was universally present? Probably not. It would be the norm. What you term miraculous is not the norm. But, if you truly consider the awakened state of consciousness, that *is* a miracle of integration, of love, of depth and harmony. That miracle carries no gender or time allotment.

Consciousness and awakening continue to unfold. So stop worrying whether you are going to make it. You cannot help but make it. You may not make it tomorrow, or the next day, but you *will* awaken in your true Self. There is no one there to hold you back, save you. There is no one saying, "You can't do it. It is not for you. Maybe next time around - another two or three embodiments." That kind of resistance you create because you do not believe you are worthy. You do not believe that somehow God can love you in the state of consciousness that you now have.

41

How can God not love you, since you are part of the Divine? Do you love your fingers and your toes? Would you cut them off? Would you say, "I don't want them, they don't serve me?" That would be the same as God saying to you, "I don't love you." You are the fingers, the toes, the eyes, the mouth, the feet, the movement, the expression of consciousness of the Divine. Each in your own way. Each in your uniqueness. And yet collectively, as one body of energy. The body is unified. It is whole. It is complete. It does know all of its parts.

In your body you may not always be conscious of everything going on, yet your body is fully conscious. Each cell has consciousness. Each cell is aware of the Divine. How do you think healing is effected? The patterns that are there are in residency, you might say, in the Divinity that each cell carries. You are a Divine being having a bit of a vacation from the knowingness of your Divinity, so you can play the game of not knowing. But the vacation is about over! [laughter] And as vacations are universally nice to embark upon, and quite often nice to come home and let go of, I think you are now coming Home.

You will let go of that particular brand of vacation called "not knowing who you truly are," and you will reunite with Home consciousness or Divinity. You will reunite with the awareness of who and what you are, what you have chosen to do, what you want to do and why you have done what you have done. In so doing you can love yourself for what you are. Not for what you might have done, or should have been, or think you want to be, but what you are now, in the now. That is all you have; the Divinity that resides ever before you, in you, and through you.

In the past, in the present and in the future, that Divinity is resident. You might say the linkage with the higher Self is absolute. You cannot be unlinked. The consciousness of that

42

linkage is another situation entirely. You can easily become unconscious. A quick way to do that is to sit and watch television. [laughter] I tease you a little. Some programs are good, but is it not a way to "zone out," relax a bit, let go of the thoughts of the day? Often, if there is any nagging worry, perhaps you let go of that. But sometimes in the same frame of thinking, there is what you might call a nagging point of enlightenment - nagging only to the personality not wanting to accept it.

Do you feel the Spirit sometimes approaching you in deep love and support of your process, yet you cannot be bothered? Has that happened to you because you do not think you are worth it? Or you are feeling a little tired and you do not want to think about meditation, or integration, or contemplation? So you say, in a sense, "Go away. Don't bother me, I am busy watching television." I tease you a little, but I want you to think of the ways that you keep yourself from knowledge.

Do you bury your sorrows in food? Do you bury your knowingness in food? That is easy to do. You have done it in many different ways. Each of you has your pet addictions. I do not want to step on toes and I don't want you to get mad at yourself for having such pets, but think about the ways that you feel clear.

How do you feel clear? When do you feel clear? Are you in nature enough? Do you feel the clarity of your body when your diet is relatively refined? Do you have a lot of fruit, vegetables and live food - vital energy food - or do you busily supply the body with a lot of dead food that makes you feel sluggish?

Food is not your god. It is not the road, ultimately, to happiness. You can be a food fanatic, eating all the right foods, yet still be miserable. But it is nice to get clear with what the body wants. It is nice to get clear with what the consciousness desires.

43

Spend the time to honor yourself in those processes. Become quiet. Let there be a time of meditation - of prayer. Let there be a time of sharing with others in joy. Let there be a time of laughter, and some frivolity. Let there be a time of touching the earth. Let go of all your thoughts of Spirituality upon occasion and just be very "normal" - maybe have a beer with friends or something. You do not have to be intensely focused on your awakening all the time, because that gets in the way, strange as it may sound. Too much intensity can get in the way, and paradoxically at the same time, the inner desire that you carry *is* the motivating factor.

If the quiet, deep desire is to experience the Divine, that is the most important. Let go of the feeling that you are not worthy. Do not work at it so hard. If you are worthy, do you have to force it? You do not have to open the doors of heaven with dynamite. It will come to you. It will witness to your being. The Spirit will give you inspiration. You will feel your love going out to others in their need. If someone comes to you with a question, perhaps an innate answer will come. Perhaps you will feel the need of their counseling process and you will go forward with it - move from the heart.

Do not be frightened by not knowing an absolute answer in those situations. Share your process. Share what has given you insight. Speak from the wisdom that will be natural to you. You will feel the resonance with another when it is correct. What a joyous opportunity then, to feel an awakening for both of you. See the need of another as a door to your own progression - your own sharing. Witness the larger need of the planet. It is so seriously in need of love, of healing, of compassion.

Rather than becoming depressed because you see the need so strongly, begin to think, "Where there is need, there will be a fulfillment. Where there is the need of the planet for well-being and insight, there will come those to serve that need." What a wonderful time to be in the body, as crazy as it sounds. It is a wonderful point of integration, of deepening consciousness. It is a point of allowing you to step beyond your personal limitations and touch that high state of clarity that you have deemed the higher Self, the inner teacher, the awakened state of consciousness.

As you desire, as you move, as you manifest, so shall it be. It will continue to unfold and reward you with its grandeur and its sense of unity. Stop thinking you are nothing, and start realizing you are everything!

Turn around some of the old ideas of Spirituality. They may have served at different points in history, but some are severely blocking you. God is not going to "get you" if you do not belong to a special church or organization. Heaven is not denied to anyone. The only denial is by self, because of the fears, the doubts, the self-imposed limitations, the belief in the small thought that you are not worthy. Let go of that thought. You are as worthy as anyone.

Look upon the man Jesus, or others in whom you have found deep inspiration. They are not, in their essence, different than you. Perhaps a little further along on the path. But their essence is yours and your essence is theirs. Let it be. Let it be so. In that way joy comes, and a deep sense of satisfaction that you have moved through life. So move through life joyfully, having a sense of the deep adventure that comes as you approach your own Divinity.

Everything else is secondary to the Divinity that you investigate within self and others. What more important area of life is there to consider? Nothing is as important. Nothing else gives lasting value. The true sense of Self is found in that dimension of reality you term the heart, the soul, the deep levels of consciousness which embrace everything else.

45

Think of the simple things that bring joy. Embrace the simplicity of the process and let it build from that. Let each step bring something new. Do not grow so impatient. Rather, enjoy the steps, the process as it comes. Join with others in so doing. If it feels a little empty just with self – wonderful; join with others as they also move to deeper levels of their integration, their sense of trust, and their desire for compassion. Both to experience and to share. You catalyze one another and enhance the overall energy available to you.

Think on these things in their simplicity. Let not yourself feel at odds within your being. There is *always* a way out. There is always a way to step beyond the limited mind. Know there is always a way to step back and let that part of the mind be observed and witnessed in its presence, but not adhered to as the sole structure of your universe. It is a small part to be integrated, to be that which you love and make friends with. But do not give it too much responsibility. The Self you seek has ultimate authority in all things you endeavor to unfold.

We will now look at your questions.

*I have experienced resistance to doing hands-on healing work. Is there a past life fear I should release in order to do the hands-on?*

Oh, I think just practice. You get past fear by practicing that energy so the fear begins to dissolve. Perfect love creates a place in which no fear can reside. The essence of healing that you call the laying-on-of-hands or absentee healing is, in its essence, love. So no fear abides in those places. Gently go forward in the world. You will do fine.

*I am sitting here feeling frightened a bit and I am not sure why.*

I think you're worrying about whether your grounding to the planet will be strong or not. You're speeding around a bit, feeling the energy of the city and such not nourishing you now. You need a little more sense of, "Yes, I can go out. I can find the leaves that drop in the fall. I can find the joy of nature in winter. I can do the things that nourish me in that environment, and know that that will support my beingness, my body, my consciousness." In no way is it an accident that you have been hungering for that lately. You have been hungering for that, haven't you?

*Yes, I have.*

That is not an accident. It is a way of the self-knowing that comes to share with you what would make you happy. Not as the absolute happiness of life, but a direction of travel, a direction of movement, a direction of your thought, your inquiry. Ground the energy. It will show you. You will feel it. You will have the knowingness. It will come.

*I like so many methods of healing and giving to others, I am not sure what form to utilize.*

Generic form! [laughter] It is called allowing compassion to form. The variety of ways that it manifests is part of the fun and excitement. Overall, let the compassion flow. The heart has been opening and it feels as if it gets a little fragile at times. Send a little love to that part of your being that feels open and vulnerable and know that that is also a strength without worrying, "Am I too open or vulnerable now?"

It is our joy to share with you.
God bless you.

47

# Meditation

*Take a moment for your own healing,*
*your own integration.*

*Feel the energy within you.*

*Sense the light of healing flowing into you.*
*Receive that sense of energy.*

*Touch the deep place of your own knowing.*
*Know that ever you walk in the light of the Spirit.*

*The deeper Self will continue to manifest*
*and deepen your unfoldment into life.*

*Allow yourself to sit quietly for a moment*
*with these thoughts.*

Chapter 5

# Relationship To Guidance And The Higher Self

*God bless you.*

*It is our joy that we might share with you
the knowledge that you walk not alone.*

*In your daily consciousness
there is a constant activity of interchange
between you and your thoughts with others.*

*Some of those are others in the body,
those to whom you feel particularly close.*

*Some of those thoughts are with those
you might call your teachers,
who are not in the body,
but who are working with you all the same.*

Much of this interchange is not in the daily mind at a conscious level. It is just beneath the surface. Sometimes you tap into that deeper level and are aware of interchanges between you and others. You may even feel at times a bit dislocated, as though you are also somewhere else, which you may well be. To the outer mind that seems a little strange. To the inner mind it is no problem, because you are, in your multiplicity of selves, able to exist simultaneously on many dimensions at once and do it all with the proper perspective. And you may question then, what is the proper perspective?

First of all, it is to recognize that this body that you have, this physical vehicle, is indeed a temple. A rather fine temple with highly developed centers of awareness that you have termed chakras, with the very deep ability to bring forth energy. And as you are able then, to master impulses that would pull the body down and you bring the body's energy up, you find the temple serves you even better and will continue to do so.

You may think that as you grow older, the temple should grow decrepit. Why should it grow decrepit? It will age, of course. In time you will perhaps find that you do not have to age at all, but most of you are now so "advanced" in your thinking, you think that is impossible. When you get less advanced and believe it is possible not to age, you will not age. But that is a moot point. What is important for you now is to feel the growing awareness of the physical temple, and in that way, honor your own process and allow more love, more joy to come. That process can continue until the time you choose to leave the body in the way that you call death.

The body can become more refined. It can become more and more developed as an energy flow, as a point of consciousness in the universe that is uniquely you and yet links with others. You begin

50

to sense how deep your consciousness is. It is as the river flowing into the ocean. First you might think you are the little trickle of water running down the face of the rock. Then you begin to think, "Aha, maybe I am the creek" - a little more water. Then finally you begin to feel, "Aha, I am part of the river." Perhaps you are now somewhere on the river. Finally you will become aware that you are also part of the ocean. It all has been true. You can simultaneously be the little drop of water, the creek, the river and the ocean.

You can even be the fog in the air. You can be the clouds before they become rain. You are all of that. You are, in the extended state of your being, the Universe. The Universe is you. You breathe out and breathe in the Universe. The Universe breathes out and breathes in you. You create in your thoughts and your desires that which shall come. Not at the level of the conscious mind, but at the level of the deeper mind.

Rather than worrying about how that is, and whether this is a word game, or whether the pictures are true, what is important is how you feel about yourself. Are you still caught in the confusion of the outer mind that has taken on the programming of society that says, "No, I am not good enough. I have not tried hard enough. Other people don't like me. I don't like me. God doesn't like me. And if I feel really guilty, maybe God will be happy that I am feeling so guilty."

Think about those thoughts. God is not an energy of guilt. God is not an energy of limitation. God is an energy beyond words. God is an energy of love and compassion that touches you in every fiber of your being, every aspect of your consciousness.

Every level of your multiplicity is permeated by the Divine. As you become aware of the water, the stream, the river, the ocean. As you become aware of yourself in that sense of a broader self, you also become aware of the trouble spots, the little eddies and currents that you want to clear up, and you bring love into those areas.

Some of them are quite interesting. You begin to find that you can bring love into the eddies and currents of other people's lives. You begin to find that as you do so, it is not your love so much as that which you channel. You can look at the channeling process in many ways. You can think of it as the higher Self or as the Universe moving through you, as the Christ Mind being present. You can think of it as a particular teacher working through you. It does not matter how you want to describe it. The important thing is that joy and love and well-being comes, and that is the nature of creation.

Deep level creation brings harmony, brings adventure, and brings a style that is your own since you are unique. And yet it brings the content that is universal, for it is not different from one source to another. If you drink water out of this faucet or that faucet, you still drink water. It does not matter what faucet you turn on, out comes water. It is important to notice however, that you can make the water into tea or coffee, or a chocolate drink if you want; you can give the process a different color - a different taste.

That is life. Life has different colors, different flavors, different tastes. Yet behind the differences it is the same - the same process. So let go of the monkey of the mind for a time. Let go of the feeling that you have to be separate from others. Let yourself embrace the fact that the Universe is limitless.

Where you have needs, those needs will be met. Let go of your worry about them. Let go of your need of control. You do not need to control your life or anyone else and you certainly do not need to control the guidance that comes to you. It will flow in your time of need. It will flow in the time of your quest. It will flow when you offer assistance to others.

It will also remind you of balance; how to continue to love yourself, how to treat the body with wisdom, how to find that you are part of the deity you seek. God has never left you. God has always been present, but you have allowed yourself to be unconscious. That is all. You are simply waking up again. You have gained in your unconscious state. That may sound strange. It may sound like a paradox. But you have gained through your unconsciousness. You have gained the ability to see yourself as separate. You have gained the ability to experience yourself as separate. That has built individuality for you.

But it is no longer necessary. You have an adequate supply of individual uniqueness. Now it is time to allow the absorbing of consciousness, the recognition of unity, the being both separate and together. Play with that division. Know that it is there for its own purpose, yet you can move through it and past it. And know just as there is the division between the inner and the outer feeling of self, there is the division, seemingly, between the physical and non-physical dimensions. That too, you can flow with.

Also become conscious of being a Spiritual entity, free to travel the Universe in whatever way you want, in whatever way serves you. You have a body, but you are not limited by the body. The body is the temple of your consciousness so that you may experience the physical dimension where mastery comes very quickly.

Why the flesh? The flesh is mastery. Why not the Spirit? Can the Spirit not gain mastery? Yes, it can. But it is a slower process. It is a little funny to talk about time, but it is a slower process in the Spirit. In the body, because you have more resistance, you have to

53

strengthen your muscles more. You have not the ease of overview that comes in Spirit. Yet as you bring it into your body's consciousness, you have gained mastery. You have gained something that is unique unto yourself and yet can be shared, always.

Whether you are in this planetary system or some other school or college of learning in some other part of the Universe, it is not a different curriculum. The essential lessons are the same. They are about learning compassion and patience, learning uniqueness and individuality and learning unity. Those are the things you move through.

So take up your own resistance. If you want to call it a cross, take up your own cross of resistance and give it love. Carry it forward. Let it see the light of day. Let it see new horizons of consciousness. Let that resistance dissolve. You have so much love to receive and give. You have just begun to feel the essence of your being. It will come stronger and stronger. And though there will be points of sadness or sorrow that come as you unfold, the essence of unity will carry you through; as waves of the ocean form with wind to create a storm, but the ocean remains the same. And if somebody else is having a storm, maybe you can calm their waves and feel the joy that comes with that.

Much happiness is on the horizon for all of humanity. But it is there for you to absorb now. Not to wait. The world seems to be in a time of conflict. To the outer mind it would look that way. Yet to the inner mind it is in a cycle of rebirth, of regeneration, of deep initiation. Collectively you are awakening. It is a time of new horizons becoming present. Not in the past or the future, but now, in the present.

It is our deep joy to share with you. In whatever way we may assist

54

your process we would be happy to do so. Perhaps you have those ideas formulated that you term questions, which are in a sense your own truths half-revealed. For to have the question is also to have the answer, but you may not quite have the answer pulled out. Maybe we can dislodge your answer a bit so you can grasp it.

*I found what you said about growth being slower in the Spirit quite interesting. Can you say more regarding that process?*

The awareness you have gained by coming into the body builds mastery. This mastery is based on the evolutionary patterns of other lives that you bring into focus, that are a mystery to the outer mind. Talent, certain levels of knowledge, certain things you take for granted in yourself are your strong points. And there are also areas you may consider weak points that you are working to unfold, to heal, to clarify. You move into greater mastery because you are working with so many elements, yet you are not fully conscious. In the Spirit you could work with the same elements, but you would be conscious.

*Wouldn't that make it faster?*

It would make it faster in one sense, but as an example; if you take an examination and you have the textbook there to get the answers out of, it is not truly an examination, is it? That is a little bit like being in the Spirit. You have all the textbooks there, you can find any answer you want. However, when you come in the body, you have read the texts, you have studied them, but you have forgotten you have done it. Now it is time to see if you have the answers so well integrated that they are there anyway. And when you have done that, and you have mastered the texts, you can throw away the books because they have *become* you.

There may also be certain things in the physical body you wish to

55

explore. You may wish to explore what it is to feel blind. It would be very difficult in the Spirit to feel blind, since you cannot be blind in the Spirit. But you can be blind in the body. One might wonder, why come in the body to be blind? What an amazing experience, that does not sound very nice at all. And yet it may truly be an act of mastery to overcome fear and doubt and any sense of limitation.

It may be a very advanced soul that chooses a disabled body or a limited environment to test out how much compassion may flow. And I do not even like the word "test." Let us throw that out too. Let us use the word "explore," not test. You create a limited environment to find out how much more of unlimited Self may fill the void that seems to be limited. So it is an exploration you may take in many ways.

*Does healing always help, or can you hinder somebody's karma?*

There can be times when you need to listen with wisdom to the process of another person's request. What did they ask you to do? In general, and on a very deep level, healing always helps and does not hinder, particularly if you key it in to the other person's higher Self. But there may come a point in your own experience when you feel resistant to working with someone because you do not like what they continue to do. For example, perhaps a friend of yours finds you have the ability to take away headaches in your healing. Every night he goes out and carouses and drinks and when he has a hangover the next day he comes to you and says, "Take away my headache." This goes on for two or three months, and pretty soon you think, "I am not helping him. He is partying and carousing so he can have a good time. He is ignoring the responsibility the headache is showing him. I will not heal his headache anymore."

Then your wisdom is coming in to affect him, to help him face his own responsibility. It is always possible that there can be an imbalance with any energy. Wisdom flows then, to create the perspective on how to use the energy.

On a deeper level, healing goes in and touches the soul. And whether the body is healed, whether the headache is gone or not, the soul is touched in a deeper way and helps to bring energy to the conscious mind, so that it may cease in playing games that do not serve. For example, too much alcohol does not serve and the healing may touch the inner Self with greater love and the inner Self will be able to respond to the personality and say, "Ahhh, I have this love in me. I do not need the alcohol to feel love and to escape my misery. The love is transforming what I call my misery and I am loving myself. I do not need the alcohol." That is the healing.

The headache may still be there or it may go. The outer mind may think no healing happened unless the headache went away. Generally it goes, but that is the way of healing; it operates on different levels of consciousness and if you want to experience the full value of healing, then you need to be open to see the various levels of consciousness that are touched. Then you have wisdom. It always works.

*If you want to send love and healing and somebody doesn't want to open up to it, do you try and force it on them?*

No, no, you never force. You never give up and you never force. What you do is be very sneaky! [laughter] You do not send love to the personality that has resistance. You send the love out to the Universe and ask the Universe to effectively distribute the love in the way that is most appropriate. So you let go of your expectations of results. Let the love find its proper way and time and place to go into the life of the other. Then the healing works just fine.

It is a way of letting go of your expectations and yet letting the energy flow. A person may want to leave the body. You send them healing, saying they must be healthy, they must stay in the body, yet they want to leave. Better that you send healing to the higher Self. And if the higher Self wants to go, then the body makes the transition easily and the person has a very natural passing and a happy transition. That is an example. It doesn't mean everybody you send healing to is going to leave the body! [laughter]

There is a series of questions each one of you might ask yourself. In the time-honored tradition that you know as philosophy, you might ask yourself, "Where have I come from? What am I doing here? Where am I going?" You might ask, "Who have I known before that is strong in this embodiment in connection with me?" You might also ask, "Who are the teachers that work closely with me now?" Ask, "How may I know the Divine essence more deeply?"

You may also ask, "Oh Lord, oh God, oh Divinity of all that is, bless me in that which I endeavor to do to increase my awareness of Thy presence." Those words become your own prayer, your own form of searching, or seeking. But let that be the overall questing of life. And let there be specific points of questioning.

You may find that you feel resistance in knowing some things. If there is pain in your life, ask of yourself very deeply, "Why is this pain present? What in my interpretation of the situation feels painful? Where am I caught in the illusion of life? How may I see through it? How may I see the strength beyond the pain?" If you find yourself caught in old habits, ask yourself, "Why this particular desire? Why this particular habit, that I thought I had mastered? Why does it come back now?" See what new levels of insight you may gain in the overcoming of old patterns that you thought you had dropped.

Engage in such a series of questioning. Not all at once, but one at a time, focus on those points perhaps for a day, or a week, or a month. Look at such thoughts as, "What is love? What is love, truly? What is the nature of the reality of that word that we use to describe the essence of the Universe?" Quest after the awareness of love. "What is sexuality brought into focus with love? What is friendship brought into focus with love? What is the sense of deity, the sense of the Divine, brought into focus with love? What is anger or hate? What resides in myself that still responds to that point of energy? Why has it been present? What good may evolve from it, and how may I clear it, so that it no longer is part of my being, since it no longer serves me? What is the energy of awareness I seek? How may I be more integrated with the Spirit?"

You may wonder at the nature of the universe. Questing in self, also is questing in the universe. Lay in the night, opening to the stars with your vision, looking at the universe in its physical structure - its magnitude, its expansion - and know that you exist in a very small part of the universe. Let the awe or the respect, the deep feeling of the Divine, come in many ways. The mind is the builder. The questions serve you as stepping-stones. Give yourself time to receive a response, so the deeper Self - the guidance that comes - may bring answers. It will not always come in word knowledge, but it will come in knowingness.

These patterns deepen your faith in life and deepen the respect for how your existence moves forward. That pattern of respect for the process itself is a very wise way to worship. Respecting the process that life holds is a wise way to give respect to everyone. It is a meaningful way. It has deep affinity for all parts of your being.

59

You have your process always before you. You have life always before you. This is the beginning of the rest of your life. Perhaps I should say lives. It is the beginning of infinity forward. It is the point in the middle of infinity backward in which you have always existed and shall always exist, but knowingly, consciously.

The gift the deity - the Divine has brought forward to you - is your individualization into consciousness; your ability to seek and know and become at one with the creation. Become a creator in your own right. Move in harmony with Divine Mind. It is a point of respect for all of life to respect your own process, your own awakening. It is the gift at the end of the rainbow.

Gently we would close now.

# Meditation

*Sit in a moment of meditation.*

*Sense the energy present in the room.*
*Feel the energy in and around you.*

*Feel the energy of those joined with you as teachers.*

*Feel the presence of your own higher being*
*resonating within you.*
*And the awareness of the deeper quest*
*that is always fulfilled.*

*May the hand of the Divine walk with you*
*and take you into the presence of that beauty*
*in which all things are consumed*
*and brought forward again*
*in new life.*

*It has been our joy to share with you.*

*God bless you.*

# Chapter 6

# Enlightenment - The Unseen Guest

*God bless you.*
*It is our joy that we might share with you.*

*In finding joy in the sharing,*
*you may see more of your own being.*

*You live now in the timelessness of truth.*
*Even as it has always been, so it is now.*

*Though you may think you walk the way of the flesh,*
*and in your ignorance you stumble and make mistakes,*
*in a sense you are never making mistakes.*

*On the deeper level there is growth and purpose being manifested*
*in the individualization of your personality,*
*the character of your being.*

*The at-one-ment you seek already exists within you.*
*It has never not existed.*

It is just that the outer mind has its limitations, purposefully enforced by what you term the ego, or the monkey mind, to allow you a sense of individuality. Out of that struggle of individualization you call "living in the body" comes awareness. That awareness is two-fold in the sense that you become conscious of your uniqueness, but you also become conscious once again of your unity. Both are important. As the unity becomes stronger in your consciousness, be without fear. You shall remain individual in your unity. Nothing is lost. Everything is gained.

You are born to a purpose in this life, which is your own choosing. You are born to the recognition of your own deeper desires. In that process you co-mingle with others in the choices they have made. As a great tapestry of life there is the weaving and the interchange of energy building a more beautiful level of awareness.

Listen to your own inner guidance, and begin to feel how you may thrust forward in life with greater harmony. And as you so thrust, as you move forward into life in the greater search for your own understanding, life will present you with the values and experiences to let that understanding grow stronger. It shall never let you down. Life does not leave you without prospective growth. Always there is more growth potential opening for you.

You may wonder, "What is growth about? What is it to seek? To achieve? Enlightened consciousness? Why should I do that? What value is in it?" Well, needless to say the outer mind tries to paint a picture, to build heaven with streets of gold and everyone playing harps and such. How many of you know how to play a harp? Nobody's even practicing! [laughter]  And if you think about it, perhaps streets of gold would be a little hard to walk on! [laughter] Those images are analogies for something of value, but in the true image of what is Divine or heaven, it is not a place in time or space. It is not someplace you go to, and say, "Aha, here I am, finally in heaven." It is a state of consciousness which represents the inner growth you have achieved.

Outwardly that which surrounds you will represent inner growth, since the two are in harmony. Your outer surroundings and your inner state correspond. You may think that sounds a bit silly and wonder, "How can two people exist at the same time in two different states of consciousness? How can one exist next to the other, the surroundings seemingly the same, if inner consciousness creates the surroundings?" Very simple. The surroundings are your perception. They are not things unto themselves. They are the experience of your perception. One person may experience joy or sadness or sorrow, and another quite the opposite, though they are in the same environment - the same energy.

That does not mean external reality has no validity. It does not mean that there is something separate that you cannot find. There is something separate you can find. If you experience the love or the joy that another carries within them, you experience part of their reality. You may also see some sadness and tears, some sense of loss that may absolutely co-exist simultaneously with the love and the joy. The outer mind would ask, "How can that be?" The inner mind has no problem with it.

As an example, you have food in your stomach that is digesting. You place more food in your mouth. You might just as easily ask, "How can I have food that I am digesting and try to ingest more to be digested? Do I not have to wait until my stomach is empty before I entertain more food?" or, to put it simply, "If one state of consciousness exists, how can I entertain another state of consciousness?" The two co-exist quite comfortably, I can assure you, for you are complexity and simplicity combined.

You are a deeply evolving being of Spiritual dimension, and yet you are also just the simplicity of who you are. It is very complex sounding, yet quite simple in its essence. You are the majesty of the universe in your essence, unrevealed yet very much present. The doorway to the Divine lies locked within you, opening now and then to allow some of that majesty to come forth. You will find more openings. You will find more doors, more Divinity, more consciousness. Then you will cease to wonder how it is possible that you may be happy and unhappy at the same time. You will find that happiness absorbs and integrates the unhappiness, and that which you considered as unhappiness begins to resonate simply as undigested and un-finalized experience. In the finalization of experience, all things become part of Divinity, even the so-called mistakes.

It is good to practice the virtues of your own self-analysis, seeing what your inner honesty prompts into consciousness. It is also good to try the process of alluding to the Divinity as external in that you might have some devotion - knowing that it is internal too. Engage in some devotion requiring a bit of patience and true humility. It does not mean to bow down before some mighty god. It means to have a little awe of life, a little surrender, a little joy. Do not feel you have to master life with an iron fist, as though it must be beaten into submission. It takes all the fun out of the participation when you feel life is a threat. It is not.

There is nothing to be gained through fear. There is everything to be gained through love. As you love yourself more deeply, more and more you will see the Divinity present in others as well. You will see the Divinity in self, and you will know that they are one and the same - not different divinities - just one Divinity manifesting its complexity by showing its face in many different ways. Yet the essence of Divinity is one.

You may have thought many times, "I must get off the wheel of life. I must cease this cycle of birth and rebirth." I would ask you, "Why?" Why must you cease the cycle of birth and rebirth? Is it a fear of dying? You have done that many times. Is it a fear of being born? You have done that many times as well. Is it a fear of any point in between? What about the afterlife states, when you enjoy consciousness in other dimensions more clearly than while you are in the body? You have done that many times too.

This cycle of life is not to be broken. It is simply that the wheel may change shape or form for you. It may be that you would not come back into the body physically. You may elect to enjoy existence in dimensions other than this one that you call the physical plane. But will evolution stop? Of course not. You continue your process of growth and development. Does that mean something radical will change? No, not that either. You will come more into harmony and integration with who you already are. You will find more of your own essence. You will find more of the subtleties of your own insight. You will find the subtleties overwhelm you in their power.
The obvious dimension of life you call love is romantic. That is the love everyone appreciates and which sparkles up their vision. There are more subtle dimensions of life that you might not think of as romantic, which have to do with deeper trust, deeper faith, and the process of existence. They do not take you from hilltop to hilltop of experience without letting you experience the valleys. You may begin to find, as with the waves on the ocean, that the ocean is one ocean, though the waves are seemingly separate from one another. The subtleties may grow strong, and in their presence you begin to understand people more deeply.

It is that unconscious level of life waiting to be revealed that is largely responsible for your fears, your doubts, your frustrations. As that is worked through and becomes more clear, that inner dimension is revealed in all of its power. The subtlety of consciousness will never cease to amaze you. The interplay that comes into focus as you begin to appreciate yourself and others in the subtlety of your own growth will be a constant joy and delight.

It is a refinement process. It is not going out into the wilderness to slay a moose, coming back as the mighty hunter. That is a romantic form in your thoughts. Is it not more powerful to go into the wilderness of your own consciousness and find there some large fear and bring it back, tenderly laid to waste, no longer present? Having examined and seen its presence, you can let it evolve, let it change, let the strength come, so that you no longer have that fear which filled up some of the empty places you have shied away from. Then your insight is deepened and your growth is strengthened. That is the mighty huntress or hunter.

The stronger way to find out who you are is to see the fears coming. Let them come into the light of your consciousness. Let them be examined and see their presence not as real, but as grounded in the thought that somehow you are incomplete. You fear that there is not enough love, that there is not enough joy, that God somehow does not love you, that other people snicker behind your back at things you do, that you are caught in self-criticisms. With such active chatter, you have a full-time occupation just making friends with the monkey mind. But it is not a monkey of vengeance or something to fear. It is your own consciousness returning again and again to be met and understood in new ways. It is your own consciousness slowly refining the patterns set down even in previous incarnations.

Finally, it is your own consciousness you are revealing to yourself as you learn to love others more deeply. To see the Divine, to see the God or the Goddess in them, to begin to recognize their individuality and their unity with you. So you say not, "*I* am in the heart of love," as though you were somehow separated from your

68

fellow being, but that you begin to see *everyone* as in the heart of love. Then you can respond more deeply to who you are and to your own wisdom.

Think of the unfoldment you move through in psychic or Spiritual dimensions. There is much room for rapid advancement. As you begin to see yourself more clearly, you will understand empathy, you will understand the sensitivities that come and go, you will understand how you may know and feel the heart of another so strongly.

You also see some of your own fears represented in the thoughts of others. Perhaps as you help them clear their fears, you clear your own. It is a nice way of growth - to be able to share. It is also important that you find time to be alone - to integrate within yourself. It is important that you suggest that the higher Self be more present. For in your request, if it is truly your desire, it comes into focus. Perhaps not always as you expect or assume, for enlightenment wears no clothing - it is invisible, but when it happens you know it is present.

Enlightenment is the unseen guest that is always available to join you at your meal - to sup, to dine, to converse with you - if you so desire. You can never be alone in the sense that your word means being separate, for alone means to be unhappy. You can be alone in the sense that you are not with others, but you are not then lonely. You are just alone. You do not have to be miserable. You can be happy with yourself. What a marvelous gift. Ultimately you begin to find that you are one with everyone else and then the dance of your joy is such that you have your individuality that you can share in your unity with them. The interchange - the process of living life - that is your process.

You are not Divine by accident. You are not Divine because you

69

have done something worthy to be either accepted or rejected in the field of Divinity. You are Divine because every portion of your being resonates with God-consciousness. One day the subtlety of that will quicken the outer mind to the extent that you cannot deny your Divinity, for it will become the fulfillment of life you have sought in so many ways.

Gently honor the Divinity that is present within you by simply loving self as well as others. If you find mistakes coming, be patient. You will move through them. If you find old judgments and criticisms coming, bring them up to look at, and then let them fall away as dust, because they are as dust when you have understood them.

So much of what you experience depends on your own personal viewpoint, your own personal will power, your own personal deep desire. Do you desire to be miserable? All of you would say, "No, of course not." But look within. Is there not sometimes a hidden set of desires that says, "I am not worthy to be Divine, therefore I choose to be miserable?" That is old programming coming to light to be clarified, to be transformed.

When the mind is actively critical of others, notice that it is truly being critical of self. When love is happening for others, so it is also that love resonates within self. And you may become a vehicle that love radiates through, because the door has been opened by your own love of self. That is not a selfish act. It is a beautiful way of integration, coming to your senses, waking up, becoming conscious as a Divine being.

Do we make it hard in words? Do we make it sound like a difficulty - such a struggle to undergo or go toward Divinity? You cannot be more Divine than you already are. You can be more conscious of it. It can be a subtle shift in a moment, or a subtle

70

shift that takes a long time. Either way the shift will come. In the time that you call time, it may seem long. In the time that your consciousness on the deeper level calls time, it is not long at all. You live in a time of great awakening.

Take the time to be with yourself. Take the time for a little devotion, a time of prayer and meditation each day. Continue with the evolution of your work and how you might look within. Perhaps through dreams, guided imagery, healing, or asking for deeper wisdom. Those are outer attributes on which you may focus. And then they become inner - no longer outside yourself. Let there be notice of the grounding of the body; feeling the planet, feeling the wholeness of your body, noticing the foods that do not leave you satisfied.

Most of all, have joy in the simple things of life. In the past, traditionally, you have focused on what shall eventually be - always expecting the rainbow to bring you the pot of gold. Notice that your hand contains the pot of gold and the rainbow radiates out from you. No searching is necessary. It is already present. Hold that image of the rainbow. It allows you to begin to trickle out the gold to others and that pot will remain full.

We would be happy to share with you in that which you call questioning - which in a sense is a statement of your own knowing coming back to be reflected. Even when you think you do not know, the answer is already there. Before you can ask the question you have the answer, but your outer mind carefully camouflages and screens the answers. So we will give you your reflection back.

*Can you tell me about my process and how I can be more clear?*

Well, we can give you general directions, but your own desire is often limited because you think you do not deserve enough. Why

71

don't you ask the universe to bring you whatever it is you most deeply desire? Ask to have the conscious mind more awakened to the deeper mind and the desire that exists there. Then you are not frightened by what you desire and you will begin to expect that the universe works; that life flows in you and through you, *and* that others will come to share who will be friends. You will find your consciousness not limited to just a few, but that there are many who are of similar vibration - similar search, you call it. Find more joy. Focus on your own meditation. I think that will give you some of the answer you seek.

*Sometimes I feel very close to my teachers and sometimes I feel I am losing them.*

Allow that to be. That is okay. It is like the waves on the ocean. Closeness will come more often. It is not just to find your teachers, you understand. They love to assist you but they are not going to be there each moment in the way that you expect. They will always be attuned to you. They will also show you your own beauty, which you did not expect.

*How do I best integrate what I have learned at this workshop in my work?*

By staying in your heart as much as you can. Feel your own body as a physical temple and recognize the power that grounding to the planet brings. Begin to see the accessibility of your own mind to deeper states of consciousness to enhance the daily work - the daily activities - so that you bring all of it in.

It does not mean you meditate while you are making decisions all day long in the sense that you set aside a special meditation. It does mean that you can be in a gentle state of meditation throughout the day, feeling the inner harmony. Try to work that into the outer life as much as possible. It is like sitting on eggs until they hatch. [laughter] You do not keep looking at them each day and think, "Aha, has this one hatched yet?" You just come and sit and they will hatch. So you sit in the inner thought of what you are hatching, what you are bringing into development.

*Could you give me some advice about my meditation?*

If you have many meditations that you have stylized into forms, which one gives you the deepest sense of being at ease with what is? That would be important - a grounded meditation. You have a strong longing to go deep in the Spirit, and that is very important. But you need to also be with the body, with the planet, with your time in the flesh as equally balanced in comparison to the meditation.

You do not have to meditate 24 hours a day. Give it five or ten minutes here and there if you like. Give it - oh, rarely would we say this to anyone - but occasionally, two to three hours may serve you, perhaps once or twice a month. But much of the time, about fifteen-twenty minutes, maybe a little longer would be fine for you. The long meditation periods you may set aside as a special form to allow a sense of your own deepening Divinity.

*My question is about my teachers. I have an Indian male teacher and a female teacher. I feel that the Indian teacher is coming through pictures and the female is more from intuition.*

Why don't you just think of it all as of the higher Self? That simplifies the process. And amplify that knowledge with the thought that your teachers also share and acknowledge their sharing of energy. But it does not matter who gets the credits. Ultimately it is God, it is Divinity, it is the higher Self within you and around you. So you don't have to worry about stylizing the

73

meditation into left and right hemispheres of the brain, or such as that.

I think we should go now. It has been our joy to share with you. Good evening and God bless you.

# Meditation

*Visualize the energy within you*
*reaching deep into the earth*
*and also into the heavens.*

*Two things to ask for:*
*That you might feel your own guidance*
*very clear and deep*
*in those things that are important.*
*And that you might witness*
*and be more present*
*with the conscious mind*
*making contact with the deeper mind.*

*Let the mind begin to let the energy flow*
*around the room*
*from the left to the right,*
*as waves moving.*

*Ask to feel the presence of one of your teachers,*
*gently coming to be with you.*

*Know you are guided.*
*Life is your lover.*
*The heart of happiness dwells within you.*

*God bless you.*

# Chapter 7

# Discovering The Warrior Within

*God bless you.*
*It is a joy that we might share with you.*

*For you are opening*
*that broader door to the universe.*
*To seek out the wisdom of the Spirit.*

*To find the doors within your own being*
*that allow you to see life*
*as an unending process.*
*To see that death and birth*
*are but doors to the physical dimension*
*with which you continue in other dimensions.*

*Reflect on the unendingness of life.*
*Begin to value those things which have worth.*

*For those things which are of the Soul or the Spirit*
*will give you riches beyond number.*
*Those things of the body may give valuable experience,*
*but if they are limited to only the outer desire,*
*then hungry shall you be.*

*For the inner hunger*
*will continue to exert its influence*
*and bring you to know*
*your own strength of purpose and will.*

*It will continue to open doors for you*
*until you find that which you meet in others*
*is also that which you meet in self.*

If you find ego in others that irritates you, look within. Is not your own ego irritating you? If you begin to find love in others, look within. Is there not the gift of loving self coming into focus? And when you have found enough in others to reflect that the same process operates within you, begin to open the doors to the welcoming of the Spirit in your life. Ask that you might have deeper counsel, that you might more deliberately seek to be a channel. That you might, in your own way, reflect on the creativity that flows through you. And that you might, in your own way, welcome the power of nature to come forth and present to you the gift of this body, being home on the planet.

The body you have is not isolated from your Spiritual consciousness; that deep sense of knowingness that you are part of the planetary consciousness, the knowingness that the gift of life is given, the temple has been awakened. And you are one with the infinite Son, with that infinity of Son, or of Christ consciousness dwelling within all humanity.

Some have awakened it and know of their Sonship. Others would doubt in the outer mind that it is at all possible. Not only is it possible, it is the greater reality of your existence. So seek to know those realities in ways that will allow you the feeling and the freedom of courage and self-conviction. Find the counsel of the Spirit as a daily active guidance. Drink deeply of meditation, of prayer, of reflection in areas of your own development. You may also share with others in their growth, for it is not enough to grow alone. You want to bring your friends, your fellow beings with you, and they the same with you. So you arrive as a happy family of life, giving unto itself. It is not so much the bloodline, but rather the deepening friendship that shows you your family.

Ultimately, in the depth of your being, lies the knowledge that all humanity is part of your family. But it is sufficient to find those of similar vibration, similar interest and consciousness - not that they must think the same as you - and similar energies that you draw unto one another so the joy of life may be made manifest. In so doing, the Spirit of your own counsel may grow strong, and you may, in your own way, come to witness the power of your conviction, the wisdom of your consciousness - that which you would term the warrior.

What does being the warrior mean? To fight wars with others? That is simple. You have done that many times before in other lives. Did it give you consciousness? Did it give you enlightenment? If so, why are you back in the body? I do not want you to get too self-critical, but I am confident you will find that fighting with others has served you little. Perhaps it has instilled some sense of courage within you. That may be the value that it has brought. But it has also brought the anguish of knowing, on a deeper level, that, "I would not do this, this is not part of my essence."

Mankind now stands - as you think - on the brink of disaster. And yet in the awakening consciousness that comes, more and more will find the power of love such that they have no fear to go forth and say no to war. To say, "I will not fight. I will be a warrior of love. I will not kill my brothers, my sisters. I will be a warrior equating my own well-being to theirs. I will not stand aside in the face of injustice. I will insist, with my own personal will, that the will of others be honored, that humanity cease in its consciousness of war and welcome the consciousness of peace, the power of love to come." Such may be your convictions, such may be your counsel.

Yet the words we speak must come out of your own heart in whatever form they take. Not words of injustice being met by injustice. That is so easy. Everyone can do that. It is very easy to grow angry in the face of anger. It is much more powerful to grow loving in the face of another's ignorance that you call anger. Deeply loving, not loving in the sense of swallowing and saying, "Oh my golly, I should better be loving, because that is what I am supposed to do."

That may be the start. That may prime the pump. That may get the flow of energy moving. But on a very deep level in your own integration, the power of love reigns supreme. It comes as an organizer, a factor within your own life to bring balance. It comes in your life as communication, to reach out and teach and share and be as the student and learner, all at once. It comes in the infinity of your wisdom that flows.

Love comes in the modesty of your own sense of humility in the light of the miraculous flow of energy through you that you term healing. You see that you of yourself did nothing. The Spirit moving through you did all things. Yet honor your part in that process. That might then be called the warrior. To honor life. To honor the victory of consciousness over ignorance. To honor the power of love over anger and hate. To honor the power of your own being over your resistance.

It may sound dramatic to use the strong terms of love and hate. What about "like, dislike?" Have you ever thought about your "slight dislike" of self, and how that creates all manner of irritations in your life you do not need to experience?

I am not suggesting that life must flow smoothly with no surface irritation. The outer mind will always find a way to feel irritated, but what about the joy? What about the undercurrent of excitement and love for yourself and your own process that comes with the discovery of guidance, that comes with the thought that the world is opening up and you can do something in your own way, to be part of that opening?

Where is the adventure - the delicious sense of adventure? Where is the sense of new discovery in meeting others for the first time, yet knowing within you have known them before? It is not an accident that this person comes into your life. It is not an accident that their hunger seems to match much of your own. In such ways you can deeply grow. In such ways you can deeply share and begin to find all manner of good things coming into your life.

The outer mind would say, "Good things, hmmm, that must mean a lot of money, fancy automobile, nice house." Those are nice things. Things have value. They may show you the abundance of Spirit if you see them as way showers on the path to show you the true configuration of energy, the true abundance that life may bring you. But do not be enslaved to your possessions. Do not let them own you. There is the freedom.

If all disappeared of your ownership of things, you would still be you. You would have essentially whatever you have in the way of your own experience. Your own inner Self is still present. Nothing can take that from you unless you take it from yourself. *You* cannot even do that if the thought be known deeply; you cannot take yourself from yourself, but the outer mind *can* convince itself that there is no self present. Of course there always is, but the outer mind then experiences pain and suffering and separation.

Why not let go of the pain? Why not embrace the being that you are? Then your equation of life is not measured by external events alone. It is measured by inner progress, process, love flowing; enlightening you, bringing you sound advice, deep wisdom - having a lot of fun in the process. We want to emphasize the fun. A lot of joy comes. So be gently reminded of the Spirit, of the things you would know. Ask for counsel that it may come.

Let yourself be a warrior in the true sense of finding love opening before you as a way to deeper life. More adventure. More true bravery. More true connection with the planet. In such ways you will empower yourself and you will empower others. This is not to say power over, but power *with* others. The empowerment of the Spirit present within you and without, flowing from within to without. Owning the love others have for you, that you may be more in love with life's process. It will give you abundance if you will allow it. Deep abundance will come.

Think on the simplicity or complexity of your desires. See where they lead you. Do they bring more adventure? Do they bring you into deeper contact with your inner dreams, your sense of Self-awakening? Do they show you how gentle the Spirit may flow, how powerful the healing may come, to gently turn the mind out of its illusion of separation? Such things are there for the deep asking, the deep desire.

The question then is, will you love yourself deeply enough to bring the desire into outer consciousness? Begin to ask that life may come to you and bring fulfillment in the true sense. That does not diminish your ownership of things - it diminishes your attachment to things. There is a big difference. Attachment binds you, whereas ownership has little to do with anything. It is the attachment that binds and limits you. If you are unattached in your ownership, then you truly have, for then you can let go. And when you can let go, you have. Think on these things.

We would not have you be without your practical wisdom. Manifest in the physical plane all you want. That is good. But manifest in the non-physical plane also. Then you have balance. Balance is a critical factor in truly becoming your own brave self. In the light of the ignorance of the outer self, be brave. Know the power of love to sustain and transform your life consciousness, your life direction, your life awakening out of illusion.

Illusion is limitation. Abundance is truth. True abundance breeds love, breeds sharing, and brings empowerment to self and others. Let true love dominate in all thoughts, in all experiences. Such is the simple way of the warrior. The heart awakened. The feet firmly planted, connecting with the planet. The hands extended to bring forward the sharing of energy.

Perhaps we might look now at some of those areas of your concern or interest which you call questions.

*What is the role of Sai Baba from India in the Aquarian Age?*

In India, there is a long tradition of those who come forth as embodiments of God consciousness. In that concept of avatar you have an understanding of Indian tradition as it might also relate to the Western mind. If in the Western mind you think of God as the universe, and all things manifesting everywhere by that which you term God, then perhaps it is difficult to conceive of the way the Indian philosophy works to allow incarnation of God in the form of man.

Each of you is an incarnation of the Divine in the form of mankind, but you are not conscious of it. Traditionally you think that it is impossible, that only one achieved such consciousness - the one you term the man Jesus. Yet he did not take credit for his personality. "These things I do, ye shall do and even greater," he proclaimed in the awareness that the Christ mind would awaken in many.

In the one you have termed the man Sai Baba, there has been that awakening of the Christ mind, the Buddha mind, and he walks in the awareness of his consciousness as one you would term avatar.

84

For many people he has been that which would awaken their consciousness to the greater potential that dwells within each individual. And there is great power and great love in Sai Baba in the consciousness deeply met from within. You understand?

*Is it true that Jesus has incarnated fourty times since he was crucified and that the last time he died was in 1943?*

Well, that is not the understanding we would give. He has not embodied since his last time in the body that you know of. But many people have been touched in their own awakening by what they might, in their understanding, see to be as the man Jesus, since that might be the highest they can conceive of.

If you experience God consciousness - what are you going to call it? If you are a Christian you may say, "I have been Jesus". If you are a Buddhist you might say, "I have been Buddha". If you are truly awakened you might say, "I have touched the Christ consciousness or the Buddha consciousness, but I am not those people in my own personal being of individual incarnations".

That would be a deeper awareness, you understand? But some would come forth saying they are Jesus. Others would come forth saying they have been Jesus. You might scratch your head a little bit in wonderment thinking, if they have been so strong in their consciousness, why are they so normal - as you define normal - now? [laughter]

I have to make a little joke, but it is good consciousness you seek, and that is what is important. Trust your own heart and stop worrying about the man Jesus. He does not want to be worshipped as a man. He wants you to worship the Christ within your own being. That is the deeper joy you can share. The greater worship. It is difficult to put into your language, since to have an avatar in the

85

body at any point in history, is to offer a point where the mind may link with Divinity and somehow sense that which is beyond division into incarnation, into embodiment, into categories. To sense the Divine behind all forms, through such individuals, is part of the gift they bring in the body.

To touch the earth with that consciousness is to form a point of contact. So it is worthy to have deep devotion, but do not overlook their teaching which always says that which is Divine lies within you. Everyone wants to put it "out there" somewhere. Everyone thinks of their Spiritual growth as such a weighty responsibility, heavy with meaning and drudgery and very serious. But look at the children around you. They are old souls with young bodies coming forth with a lot of joy. Response-to-ability - not responsibility. There is a big difference.

So respond to the ability to love. Let the Christ, the Buddha, flow through you. Let the thought of your individual uniqueness not be so important. You will retain that. You will not lose it. But how much better to receive the universe in the process. Remember, the Divine speaks to you and through you. Or to put it differently, mankind receives of the Divinity through those who have acted as channels. But the ultimate purpose of their channeling, their receptivity, their example, is to awaken each one within themselves.

By the way, the prophets, the sages, the seers, those who have been enlightened in any sense were not all men. There have been equal amounts of men and women, for the soul has no gender. But your history treats the women lightly, emphasizing the men in awakening, as in most other things. Do not believe everything your history says. Look deeper. The soul knows, soul-to-soul, what is truth. Nothing is hidden. It is a deeper level of your being. All things may then be revealed within.

*People are concerned about a big catastrophe in the year 2000, but I believe religions use "doomsday" to their advantage. Is there a "big bang" coming? Many in this room are young enough to be concerned.*

Well, perhaps not everyone is so concerned, but it is a very fine question. Some of you will forget that you were worried. If you look back one hundred years in your time of history at technology, what do you see? Tremendous expansion, is that not so? There is also a growing expansion of consciousness. And the "big bang", as it has been called by some, is simply an outer fear of the manifestation of the Spirit. The ego resists change, it does not like change, it wants to remain in control. And as the Spirit grows stronger the ego gets a little frightened.

What you have essentially is the quaking of the collective ego. And to go along with the power of mind to create, in those things you term earthquakes, the quaking of ego equals quaking of earth, if you get enough people quaking! [laughter] But as love comes more and more, which it will, then the real "bang" is love consciousness banging open. [laughter] Maybe you would say exploding. It is very powerful, in terms of the Soul's consciousness, to see such change take place in the limited span of one life - which is very brief. And that is what is taking place.

The planet is waking up collectively. So everyone gets frightened in the outer mind. And they believe in all manner of doomsday prophecies. When within there is great joy. You do have the power to clear the planet of life. In your nuclear weapons that power exists. I do not think you will use it. The probability factors are about seventy-five percent that you will not, twenty-five percent that you will. Those are not wonderful odds, but before everybody gets frightened, let me ask you, what is the worst thing that can happen? You can leave the body. So what? You would go out together, all of you, to find another schoolhouse, and create a new time of learning and growth. I do not think you will do that, with the help of the Spirit and the help of many others you may not know vibratorily yet.

There is much focus from all over the universe to allow this planet, this schoolhouse, to graduate and to bring those on it into graduation. So what you are experiencing is a waking up. What you are seeing is fear of that awakening.

Be joyous. It will not happen in a moment of time set at the year 2000. It is a translation of energy that is happening more and more. Each of you feels in your own heart the acceleration of time; the speeding up of your experience of life. Time is an illusion, so it can go slow or fast, but it is speeding up to the conscious mind's sensitivity. The growth process you are involved in - each in your way - will become more and more the growth process that many are also involved in.

See the point of your return to consciousness and take heed that you have not fear. Let joy come. Fear not the demise of the body. The body has died many times. It will last a long time or it will last a short time. That is not so important. Welcome the expansion of consciousness. Then you will love your body deeply, which will allow it to be on the planet much longer.

If you find heaven on earth, there is no reason to think you have to leave the planet to find heaven. Heaven can be wherever you are. You might as well find it within the body. That is a major overcoming of old consciousness, letting new consciousness come in. So it is a time of awakening.

*I go to workshops, read books, hear tapes and absorb a lot of Spiritual knowledge, but I find it difficult to express the Spiritual learning in my daily life among fellow human beings.*

88

To strike a bargain with yourself that you will be on a Spiritual adventure is to find the doors opening. It does not mean you have to force them. You do not have to use dynamite to open the doors of heaven. [laughter] So that would mean some gentle meditations, some activity the body loves, to feel the oxygen, the body's own resources brought into focus. It is also to begin to discover what work truly suits you - what areas of contact with others truly serves you. You may find your sensitivity increases to the point that you cannot hang out with your friends and drink a lot of beer anymore. Everybody gets frightened when I say that! [laughter]

You begin to find that there is a lot of joy in Spirit energy and you do not need artificial Spirits to make it stronger. That is not to take away the beer. You can have a beer occasionally. But the energy begins to shift patterns in your personal life. And if you honor those patterns, you are still on the adventure. If you fight them and say, "Okay, God, I didn't want this, I wanted that. How come you gave me this?" Look very much at what you think you did not want.

If you have the sensitivity to feel the pain of another person, does that mean you have to jump down in the pit of their pain and wallow in it? No. It means you may begin to find ways to assist them or allow them to assist themselves, with a little encouragement. By seeing their pain you can know what it is about and bring it into the point of knowing - having compassion but not getting lost in your sensitivity.

It is a way of strengthening your grounding process to equal the opening that you have brought through your times of contemplation, study and working with others. It is an ongoing balance that you strike over and over. I would say that for many of you, one of the increasing points of difficulty is to be in the city so much. Your body wants to be free in nature. It wants to move. It wants to enjoy nature. I cannot say in general what would be specific to each person, but seek within to have a little contact with your own Spiritual counsel. Ask, what is coming up most strongly? See how that feels. It will give you good grounding.

The power of love expressing through you - that is the deepest grounding and the greatest desire. All other things are less than that. That power will keep teaching you how you can let go of the worry mind. And you might worry a lot while that is happening, but it will teach you about that. Think of it as a psychic barrier that you are moving through. The frustrations and fears that come up, are there to be met. Just as when you go on a long fast and you clear a lot of toxins out of the body - you feel them as they leave. In your deep sense of Spiritual search there are old toxins of many lives, of half-truths and some ignorances that you are clearing out. So be a little patient. And at the same time be happily expectant of the results.

I do not think we should go further. You will each, in your own way, discover the essence of your truth. For that truth has never left you. It has always resided within and will continue to do so. The outer life you lead gives you opportunities to act as a mirror to your deeper knowing. So take those things which have value to you and see where they resonate in your own being. That is how life works.

Let go of the doubts, the fears. Do not program the subconscious mind with a lot of tension. Be aware of TV, movies and newspapers with which you feed the subconscious mind.

Begin to use the power of suggestion that the subconscious so easily accepts. By studying, reading and listening to that which contains joy, that which is music of joy, that which is visually of joy. More particularly, express your own joy with others. That is

90

very powerful. You will make the connection with your higher Self in that way.

# Meditation

*Center yourself deep in the earth.*

*Visualize yourself as a tree*
*with roots reaching deep into the planet.*

*Feeling the power of the planet as a golden light*
*coming up through your roots to nourish your being.*

*Feel the golden light of the heavens*
*flowing into the leaves to nourish the being you are.*

*Feel those who are present now, unseen,*
*whom you call teachers.*
*Feel the presence of the holiness,*
*the wholeness,*
*the completeness of the Spirit within you.*

*See yourself in a circle of light.*

*In the center of that circle,*
*see a very strong light,*
*a radiant energy.*
*Feel the deep connection of heaven and earth*
*in the center of your circle.*

*In your heart, find your deep desire*
*and present it to the center of the circle,*
*that it might find manifestation,*
*that healing and love might flow*
*into that which is your desire.*

*Ask that you might receive
that which is your deep desire.*

*May clarity for the outer mind
come in all things that you seek,
so that your heart may be glad
and love may open itself to you.*

*Be joyous.*

*God bless you.*

Chapter 8

# Why Embody?
# Spiritual And Physical Dimensions
# Of Evolution

*God bless you.*
*It is a joy that we might share with you.*

*You have been seeking to overcome the ego.*

*In this time of the body you find yourself wondering,*
*"What am I doing here?*
*Where am I going?*
*What has been before?"*

*These eternal questions come into your thoughts.*
*Yet on a deeper level,*
*you know precisely what you are doing here.*

*You are working out issues.*
*You are learning.*
*You are growing in consciousness.*
*You are meeting new opportunities*
*and beginning to discover*
*new levels of creativity.*

*You are beginning to sense*
*that the world's consciousness is shifting.*
*And that you can play a vital role*

*in that shift*
*simply by allowing deeper self-love.*

*If you truly feel love for self,*
*love for others will be automatic,*
*and you will affect*
*the state of consciousness in the world.*

This is a very important time to be in the body. A time of change - of transition from one age of consciousness into another. A great time of awakening. You may look around, wondering, "What is so special about this time?" There are earthquakes. There is war, famine, subjection of the body to pollutants and poisons. All of that is part of the cycle of birth and rebirth that you go through. You are dying at one level of consciousness, and opening to more. So the planet goes through a bit of transition, which is an outer reflection of your own inner transition. For many of you it may be a bit frightening, yet you will weather the storm. It will pass.

You are entering a new level of consciousness. It will be achieved because everyone is doing it, not just a few. You are moving forward collectively. In the roots of humanity, change is taking place. But if you read only your newspapers or look at the news media, you will see the outer form of imbalance dramatized. You will not have a view of the inner change which is not as dramatic, but which is much more important.

So, why embody? It is a good question. It is a wonderful time to embody. That would be perhaps your number one reason. Your secondary reason is that you grow quickly when you embody. It may sound strange, but in the Spirit you have so much understanding that the opportunity to grow is lessened. In the body you are more restricted so you have to rely on your inner awareness. You have to draw forth the subjective sense to bring it to consciousness. By so doing, you move against much resistance and therefore create much growth. It is a bit hard to explain in your language, but you have had the option, I can assure you, to remain behind in the Spirit. But I think you have wisely picked to be in the body, to enjoy that process even when you do not understand it.

97

Understanding the purpose of your embodiment is not just an intellectual process. When you open to that understanding of self-knowledge, it will burn in every fiber of your being as truth. It will not be something you would criticize or think, "Oh this *might* be, ho-hum, I wonder if it is true?" It will be that which lives within you. It will be that which helps to bring clarity to your motivation.

I could speak to you of some of your reasons for embodiment, but unless you are ready to absorb it, then I have limited your desire to seek it out in yourself. Then I have not given you a gift, I have taken something from you. There may be a time when you are ready and then we will speak. But just to say, "I want to know my embodiment purpose," might be like trying to understand how Beethoven wrote such beautiful music - you are given a little explanation and you think you understand how to write beautiful music.

Can you see the difference? One is a picture of the reality - the other is directly experiencing the reality. So I would commend you on your purpose for embodiment, having chosen to be here in this world at this time. It is a wonderful time, regardless of how it appears on the surface.

I would ask you to seek out, from within Self, from within your deeper knowing, a direct answer in the feeling state, not the intellectual state. Ask, "Why have I come forth? What gives me excitement? What do I feel thrilled about? What part of planetary consciousness do I most like to align myself with? What do I find interesting? What does my outer mind find interesting? What does my personality desire? What is my feeling and desire on a deeper level?"

All of those are questions you may ask of Self to help penetrate barriers to consciousness, such as fear, doubt, and frustration. Those things represent a lack of belief in your worthiness to know. When you penetrate those barriers, you begin to sense that you are Divine. You are worthy. You have the right to experience knowingness. You have the right to share that knowingness. That right is also extended to everyone else. They do not have to think just as you do, but in your heart where love is present, love is the direct means of communication. Love is the power that transcends the intellectual mind.

Perhaps we have given you something to think about; why you may have chosen to embody; what you call your karmatic purpose. Some think of karma as something negative: "I have got all this bad karma I have to overcome, so life is very difficult." That is the outer mind trying to dramatize the process. If you want it hard and difficult, you can have it hard and difficult. The universe will give you whatever you want. And if you want to call it karmatic and make it an important life purpose to move through your karma - because there is a stern, angry God out there somewhere, forcing you to do it - you can have that.

If you do not want that and you want instead to sense more of the joy and grandeur of yourself as a being in the Divine image, if you want to begin to sense through that perception the Divinity in others - what a wonderful adventure life becomes! It is much more significant to allow the Divinity of all things to be your ally, to walk by your side, to be revealed within you and within others. Begin to step aside from that old sense of limitation as to what Divinity is, and feel the influx of a deep desire for a more Divine connection. Continue to bring that forward into this time, this purpose, this embodiment, this personality.

Let it extend past the frustration level, the fear level. Let it begin to modify and heal and bring healing to the depth of your soul. So that you may feel the joy of love, the playfulness, the childlike perspective, as well as the very deep levels of insight that may appear serious, but which carry a very fine chuckle with them. You can lighten up. As you receive enlightenment, it will lighten you up.

You will begin to feel the happiness of the universe. You will begin to sense that it is wonderful to be in the body. And even when you experience some form of pain - intellectual, physical, mental, emotional - that too, you can have a bit of laughter around. Know that it is the last vestiges of the ego being reduced to a very fine nothingness, as you move through some of those points of resistance.

It is a wonderful time to be in the body. It will help if you think of those teachers who work with you as also enjoying the process. You may see that you are stubborn at times and wonder how they can stand to be with you. They see your beauty, not just your stubbornness. They see the beautiful being that you truly are. They enjoy working with you. It is not a drudgery. It is not something they must do. They gladly orient themselves into your life process to help you grow. And at the same time, they are growing. There is nothing you can do in the way of gaining experience that does not create more growth, so they grow in the bargain.

*What is the purpose of traumatic circumstances surrounding certain cultures that embody, such as the American Indian?*

Well, first of all, observe that you have experienced that type of circumstance in some life, in some form of culture. You have moved through times where man's inhumanity to man has

100

been very obvious.

Perhaps the primary purpose is that you might have more compassion. If that sounds a little strange, perhaps too simplistic, look upon the AIDS factor in your culture at this time, and look upon the slavery that fear brings. Many people living in the world now are in fear. There are many forms of fear. That is slavery also. It may not be genocide, but it takes its toll. When such events occur, your planet has the opportunity to learn compassion.

If you look upon the various levels of restriction, some more obvious - such as the American Indians having their cultures largely destroyed by the contact with the emerging European cultures - you would find that those who have left the body, including many American Indians, are not at a point in their evolution where they are prepared to be teachers in Spirit. Many have embodied again. Think very carefully about it. Perhaps you were there and you have come back in the body.

In Native American cultures there was a closeness with nature. There was an awareness of the planetary consciousness you might term the Mother, or Mother Earth. Much of that is being re-activated because your balance is such that it needs to be.

The cycle of lives present in different cultures will move you through a variety of experiences. Death, to the soul, is nothing. Death of the physical body is no more than the turning of the final page on a chapter in the book. You prepare for another chapter.

I do not want to create for you a blasé attitude toward death, to say, "Oh, it does not matter if people die or not." It is important that you feel compassion for suffering and need, wherever it may be found, but do not fear death. Death is ultimately your friend. It is a transition point - a door to another level of experience. It is just that those times of death often have more of an effect on those left behind than those who left the body.

More compassion is the ultimate goal of life, whatever form the pattern moves through.

*When groups move through suffering like that, is it for the impact it will have on the rest of humanity?*

Well, you have to investigate the reason each one makes a choice. If you look back in your own history, your own personal history, you may find a time when you were very warlike, a warrior. You may even find a time when you glorified in war, when the taking of life was sport, somehow invigorating to the ego. You may have that life sitting there in your storehouse of consciousness, and you seek to modify it with a life where you are in the environment of life being taken. You may experience the pain and the suffering that experience may bring, to help deepen your compassion.

A balancing is taking place. Some would call it karma, but I would simply call it choice, to help learn lessons which may need to be learned. This would be at the individual level. You can take and expand that. One individual may also desire to be present with a particular small group of family and friends, and they each, in his or her own way, have inter-linking reasons to be present.

For example, the Jewish citizens of Germany and other countries were largely exterminated in World War II. A question might be, what positive process could that have served? In what way could that be at all considered to be positive? The consciousness that emerged through Hitler became extremely imbalanced, it became a negativity that the world had to step forward and stop.

In the vast ignorance of Hitler's consciousness, as it finally emerged, the taking of life became so mechanical that the world was rightly horrified at the revelation of what took place. Man's consciousness was tweaked a bit, you might say, prompting a little more compassion to come forward.

The world still has pockets of such atrocities being perpetrated, from the outer mind's view. But we would remind you that from the inner mind, no one dies. Perhaps those who die actually have deep compassion for those who perpetuated their death, for they are the ones, in the deepest sense, suffering from their ignorance. It is better to be killed than to kill. It is a deep truth. No one longs to look at that in the conscious mind.

If you study the work of Gandhi, you find there an awakened state of being. He saw that ultimately human consciousness would shift if the reason for compassion was allowed to deepen. Compassion is the natural right of the soul. It is the natural state of consciousness. Lack of compassion is simply ignorance. It is forgetfulness. It is like one deeply asleep.

So you might look at the Jewish death process in World War II and see it as a way of helping to awaken mankind, which was slightly asleep.

*Does a traumatic event like that* have *to happen?*

Well, that was a very complex event. It did not have to happen. On a deeper level Hitler was a very old soul who had a major purpose to enact. Many who were part of his power structure

103

thought they would be joining a rather enlightened experience of life. However, his karmatic experience, you could call it, was heavily overshadowed in such a way that as he moved into maturity, and moved into a point of personal power, his deeper enlightenment became overshadowed by vindictiveness.

If you study the late twenties and thirties, you will find that Germany struggled in a rather vindictive environment perpetuated after World War I. The energy shifted sufficiently that Hitler's deeper compassion did not emerge and finally, you might say, gave up. Only the shell of his consciousness remained. Yet with that rather magnetic sense, you call charisma, so it became very strong in a negative sense - in the sense of emblazening the ego out of all proportion to the Spirit.

The world did need to step forward to bring a stop to that, but the tragedy did not *have* to happen. The potential was there for a quickening of the New Age awakening. It sounds rather strange, but there is a collective karma that the human race shares, not just individual karma.

Humanity will move through whatever cycle needs to be moved through, until compassion and great freedom are brought forward. Nothing *has* to happen, but the patterns are set in motion and the ways to fulfill the lack of learning, the lack of compassion, may be through pain and suffering. It does not *have* to be through pain and suffering. It can also be through joy. It is a choice each of you makes daily, moment by moment. Do you want to be in suffering, or do you allow yourself to embrace joy? Think of this; within you there is a little Hitler and within you there is Divinity. Which do you more quickly express; the ego mind in its rather obnoxious sense, or the deeper sense and the ego in harmony with that deeper sense?

104

Heaven and hell exist within each of you. Choose. Why not have heaven?

*Teacher, is it true that we more or less "promise to forget" when we embody?*

Not everyone. A lot of your young children are not so forgetful.

*Then is it programmed out?*

Well, let us examine the purpose of knowing. What serves you the most? If you come into life with remembrance of other lives it may create an imbalance. For example, perhaps you remember a time when you were the warlike individual. Could you live with that conscious knowledge? You might find yourself so disgusted, so judgmental of your past remembrance, that you would not allow yourself to blossom.

In many respects, the lack of knowingness of your past is there as a safeguard, until your consciousness is sufficiently endowed with wisdom, joy, laughter, spontaneity, a sense of self-forgiveness, and a sense of deep compassion for others. Then you can lift the veil and see what you have done before without great condemnation.

The basic purpose of not remembering is to allow the individualization process to take place.
*Are teachers such as yourself here to help expedite and speed this up?*

Of course, and so are you. You are here to do the same, in your own way. It may be obvious. It may be very subtle. But in whatever way you allow yourself to awaken, you touch others,

105

consciously or unconsciously. It is a collective process.

*Some scientists predict that people will be extinct fifty million years from now. Can we look forward to the planet going on? Also, are there life forms in other galaxies? Can we come back in other galaxies, or are we bound to this earth?*

You have all been in other galaxies, you might say, before. There are cycles of growth and evolvement simultaneously taking place throughout your universe. Where those who are embodying in connection with matter, with the material process, begin and complete the individualization processes.

The structure of the body, the form, the shape, matters little. It is the experience of that evolvement, that allowing of a conscious mind to create some sense of separation from the Divinity that is present, that allows the individualization process to move forward. That is taking place in many, many places beyond number. That which you call the UFO phenomena and such are inter-linking points with you to help in your evolutionary process. You will find that to be true in a few years - it will not be so long until it happens.

You need not worry about the future of your planet, though I would not say to stick your head in the sand and ignore the threat of nuclear war and such. Do what you can to assist, to allow opening, to allow more compassion, but do not be rooted in fear. Do not be enmeshed in the fear of what *might* happen, which then leaves you immobile and robs your energy. Have more the sense of, "Here is the challenge."

Let love come. Ask that you might be a channel for love, for wisdom. In that way, the pattern of the planet will move in the direction of the most progression. It becomes an evolving schoolhouse. And that is what it is - a schoolhouse. (smiling) And I do not think you need to worry about fifty million years from now! [laughter]

*How do we explore past lives to see what we were?*

Various ways. One would simply be your own desire to investigate more of how the process functions. Read a bit. Investigate ways in which others have stumbled across that truth; how it has come up unbidden in some, or remembered in some from the time of birth.

You can have some glimpse through a channeled state of consciousness of another, giving some of the details. I was tempted to say the sordid details, to tease you a bit! This will help you see an overview of what you have been doing. It may register as a reminder of things you already have sensed.

The hypnotic state may be used. Either self-induced or through someone else bringing forth that knowledge from the subconscious, which is a storehouse or memory bank. But I think the question is whether it is appropriate. Will it serve you? Will you value it? If it is brought forth prematurely you may not allow yourself to trust and value it. It would be helpful to state, "I would like to know whatever is of deep truth for me; what may serve me. Part of that truth I would like to understand is something of the embodiment process, some glimpse of those points in the past that may serve me. As much as I am able to handle, I would like to know."

Let that be a prayer state about once a week. Let there be a daily meditation. Then, with all that focus on remembrance, totally let it go at the same time. It may take a month or two, it may take a year or two, but that will begin to precipitate some of the states of knowing.

Notice little things, little guideposts. When you meet someone that you have not known before and they feel very familiar, it may be symbolic of their presence in your past, when you may have been friends. You may have been enemies. You may have been in some form of relationship. There will be a knowingness.

When you find that connection with another it is important to acknowledge that this is not the first time you have known another. That helps. It adds a delicious level of adventure to your life process, to see those points of opening, those unfoldments taking place.

Think about the cultures you have felt most attracted to. Think about the points of geography that have attracted you. They may also hold a bit of a key to something you have done. What cultures did you feel strongly about as a child? What stories did you like to have read to you? Was there a strong desire to know about the area of India, or Asia, or the Middle East, or the American Indians? What was your desire as a child? Often this triggers some point of past life experience.

*What if you like dinosaurs?*

That would perhaps indicate your desire to understand the depths of man's embodiment. Mankind is much longer on the planet than your scientists would think. They are slowly stretching the limits back. I think partly a sense of awe at the agelessness of life process exemplified by the dinosaur - that is what that would suggest - to feel the past, present and future as a continuum that is part of Divinity.

108

*I feel sometimes that my ego gets in the way.*

Everybody feels that. But it is good to make friends with your ego mind. You cannot beat it up. It has to be present. It has to move through the evolutionary process. Love your limitations as points of great change. That is a way of loving the ego.

*I almost go out of my way to resist change. Yet I know that once I get to the change I'm going to like it!*

That is better knowing than most people have. Most people severely suspect there could be anything to like when it comes that quickly. But it comes. Be happy with what is, and it comes quicker. More happiness allows more change.

# Meditation

*Sit now in a moment of meditation.*

*Feel free to ask those*
*who work with you as teachers*
*to be present,*
*joining with you in the meditation.*

*Begin to sense light flowing out to you.*
*Begin to sense light flowing through you.*

*A little bit of playful energy*
*is moving in and through you.*
*A sense of healing,*
*of compassion opening.*

*Begin to look inside*
*and feel the energy*
*gently swirling and circling around you.*
*Feel it moving in from the left to the right.*

*Sense in front of you a river of light,*
*a column of light,*
*moving from the heavens down into the earth,*
*as an energy flow which you become part of.*

*Gently walk the way*
*of your own deep hunger for awakening.*

*It will come.*
*The joy will come.*
*The adventure will deepen.*

*It has been our joy to share with you.*

*Good evening.*
*God bless you.*

Chapter 9

# The Meaning And Nature
# Of Embodiment

*God bless you.*
*It is our joy that we might share with you.*

*In your search to find your way back*
*to your own deeper truth,*
*it is important that you consider*
*the nature of embodiment.*

*So you do not find yourself believing*
*that somehow you are cast upon the earth*
*by the whim of fate*
*and blown around by the breeze,*
*like a leaf falling from the tree*
*to encounter whatever life would hold.*

*Rather,*
*reconstruct in your thought*
*the beginning of the birthing process*
*that you call conception,*
*and see that in the Spirit*
*you have planned the opportunity to enter the flesh.*

*You planned with those*
*who are skilled in such planning,*
*as well as the soul or the deeper Self of the parents,*
*and with others who are also planning*

*to move into the body.*

*Embodiment becomes something of a great tapestry with many people involved.*

When you have the opportunity to come into the body, you make the first link as a soul at the point of conception. And during gestation your linkage is there, overshadowing the development of the fetus. At some point there is the active portion of energy that the mother may feel as the quickening of the fetus, a sense of contact being solidly made with the physical body. Yet, in your Soul consciousness you still have not made the final link. Generally at birth you make that link, but not always. Sometimes it is prior to birth; sometimes as much as a month after birth.

So stretch your thinking a bit to include the plans and patterns you have made with others all out of free choice - out of the very deepest nature of your freedom to choose. To come into the body then is an opportunity. It is not a punishment or something you have to do. It is something you proceed with when the opportunity is present, because the Spirit can grow quickly. In the Spirit you do not have resistance, but in the body you have much resistance. So growth in the body is very profound.

Now you may feel disappointed, in your own sense of timing of where you are going and how fast you are getting there. You might feel you are not moving quickly enough, that evolution is too hard. On a conscious level you can't seem to grasp it, and yet, inwardly you are probably quietly congratulating yourself much of the time over a job well done. Of course the outer mind does not know that.

I do not want you to think you should not look critically at your life, but you do not have to crucify yourself over little obstacles you encounter where you think you failed. In exchange for the experience, you grew. Every kind of experience can create growth, if it is wisely used. Even if you make a mistake, you can use the wisdom to enhance your understanding. That is basic.

To go deeper, invite those who actively guide you to work in

115

harmony with your deeper desire. They are not there to pull strings as though one were a puppet. They are present by your free choice and your deep desire, and by their free choice and desire. In being present they allow you another eye to see your own choices more clearly. They will not dictate that you must do this or that. They will give strong guidance if necessary, but in your free choice you have many levels of consciousness. You can choose whether or not to listen.

The deepest level of consciousness is that which you term the Soul. That is the level in which you choose to embody. That is the level in which you choose to disembody. It is not an accident when you leave the planet, just as it is not an accident when you enter the flesh. At the level of the conscious mind you might think, "How can that be? Death is accidental." Yet, to the deeper mind, no accidents exist. You can see then, the difference in the perspectives of the deeper mind and the conscious mind. Which is right, which is wrong? They are both right in their respective spheres of consciousness.

In order to understand the depth of your own nature, it is important to recognize that free choice ultimately dwells at the level beyond the outer mind. That which you frequently call free choice is often just the opportunity to give a little vent to your irritation that you are not growing as quickly as you would like. "It is the fault of so and so, my upbringing, this happened to me, that happened to me," as though you were a pawn in life being pushed around by external circumstance. How much more exciting to begin to think, "Divine mind is empowering me to make the correct choices. I have an inner level of consciousness that already knows what I want to do." What an amazing adventure to begin to follow that inner consciousness. In so doing, things will at times begin to happen without effort.

You will find yourself at the right place at the right time with the right interest. You will connect with others just as you need to. You may find at times that your heart empties, out of fear, or out of pain or sorrow, and then it fills again out of the gladness of life flowing back to you. In those peak periods of extreme emotional energy you will often find a great deal of clarity counter-balancing the confusion you might think you have. Again, the deeper mind is present. The outer mind wants to disallow what the deeper mind knows, many times. You can go away from your deeper knowing, but it is a lonely path. The conscious mind feels little recognition of the true Self then. It is very lonely.

Better to embrace your higher wisdom. Embrace the deeper nature of your being. Acknowledge that the conscious mind has somewhat severe limitations. Deepen your perception to include more of the deeper mind - the feeling of the Soul. That does not always come under the label of knowledge, or - as you would term it - intellectual capacity. It may be on the very deep level of sensing. When you discover the deep nature of compassion, you have moved into the sphere of the Soul.

There is no ego at that level. The outer mind would say, "Oh, I wish I could bedazzle others with the display of my consciousness; my power, my amazing gift to heal, or my ability to speak and lecture, perhaps to channel, or perhaps to be the ultimate body-worker." Did I step on your toes? I hope not, because we would like to empower you to feel excited about all the ways you may give to others, but not to think, "I am special. I am better than others." Rather, you might think, "What a wonderful energy we all share that we can each be transformed. We can each become creative and productive in different ways." This attitude allows you to see the Soul light, the Christ consciousness, the Buddha mind, present in anyone, irrespective or whether or not they see it themselves. You can see - you can know their Divinity.

117

In that way you can fully balance your personality self. You come full circle in perception. You will not then, be caught by the outer mind's desire to be different, to be better, to be special. It is wonderful to be different and better and special, inasmuch as the outer mind perhaps needs that perceptive sense of your specialness. But when you go very deep, life becomes special. Everything becomes special. You are special and so is everyone else. That is much deeper. That is a much higher standard of consciousness. That is not to say less than that is wrong, but it is to say that less than that may be incomplete.

If you have a strong sense of ego saying you are better, look at yourself as perhaps getting out of focus. If you have a strong sense of ego saying you are not better, that you are less than, it is equally out of focus. If you have a nice, balanced ego, it might say, "Hmm, I am pretty much like everybody else and on a very deep level, we are all so wonderful. How can I pry open the door to my consciousness just a bit more to experience that wonderful energy? How can I move to a place of more natural perception? How may I feel the power of the Spirit that flows through nature? How may my compassion move me past my selfish tendencies? How may I love my own ego as though it is part of my being, not try to destroy it, and yet recognize that it is not in command?"

It is that balanced perspective that you may draw forth by asking in your prayers or meditation to communicate with others. You may feel the influence that they might share with you, as the Spirit overshadows them, to give you a message - something you need to hear. And you may do the same, so that in energy, in words, in feeling and in knowingness you may remove your outer mind from its pre-eminent role - from thinking it is in control. Then you may move back to your roots. Back to the deeper level of consciousness. Back to the place of your knowingness that transcends time.

118

This consciousness is not caught in the limited issues of one life or one personality, but rather begins to touch those many lives and see the threads of connection that link you and others. The deep connections with your friends, your family, your lovers then allow that insight, that feeling state. And you understand why you are with someone and how it is you may grow together, how love may be deepened. All of that comes as you seek your own wisdom, because it is not only yours - it is universal wisdom that through you takes on its own uniqueness. Then it is your own wisdom. But it is available for others and becomes universal as it is shared.

So you might say you have to baby-sit the state of consciousness that emerges now and then, which sometimes acts like a baby. You can be the midwife, you can be the doctor, you can be the one who delivers your own awakened state with expectancy and with joy, just as you would welcome an advanced soul into the world in the physical body. Actively seek to welcome that advanced state of your own consciousness. It is a wonderful analogy if you make use of it - to think that you are being born on the deeper level and to allow that transformation.

Think on these matters. Explore the joy in which your self-discovery may take place. It can be a long, wearisome, boring process if you want it to be. Make it hard work if you want. But why not let it be an adventure of joy? Why not let it be your favorite thing in life? Then you accelerate the process and you open to the Divine presence to awaken your consciousness with a great sense of adventure, a great sense of, "This is a wonderful time to be on the planet." Think on these things in their simplicity. They dwell within you as a deep knowing.

If you would like, perhaps we may look at your questionings. Know that ye have the answer to the question. Within you the answer is present, else the question could not come forth, but it is

119

our happiness to reflect your answer to you.

*I heard that every day another form of life on earth is extinct. You have mentioned alien life forms before and I was wondering if they know that this is happening - and if they do know, do they care? Are they going to do anything about it?*

Who do you think all those people from other planets are? Look around you. We have all existed in other planetary systems besides this one. So if you want to call yourselves aliens, you can. You are alien to this place and time unless it draws you to your heart, then you are no longer an alien. I tease you a little bit - playing on words a bit. But I want you to just re-address the question. Rather than externalizing some authority, whether from God or the heavens or angels or those in the UFO's, think about, does it touch your heart? Would *you* like to do something about it? What does your compassion tell you? There you have the answer.

Mankind, in the freedom to evolve, will not be blocked in self-destruction if it comes to that. I do not think it will, but I want you to realize that you could, if you wanted to, walk out onto the middle of the freeway and end your physical life, is that not so? That is something of the analogy to what the planetary consciousness of humanity collectively is capable of doing with your nuclear weapons. It would be a silly move, I do not think you will. But if you did, you would find another planet, make another schoolhouse, enact the same processes over again until you got it right.

More to the point of your question; there is unfortunately a loss of some of the genetic structure of that which you know in both plant and animal form that will not reappear on this planet. You have not, however, destroyed consciousness. That can never be done. You have allowed some forms to be channels for consciousness no

120

longer. You have limited that form. But other forms of extended levels of consciousness will come into focus. So there will be healing.

There will be more and more healing until finally, perhaps by the year 2025-2030, you will stop having wars. You will all scratch your heads in wonderment, thinking, "How could we have been so foolish? What a waste of energy. What a waste of talent. What a waste of intellectual and Spiritual wisdom. What a waste." You will have nurtured your consciousness to the point that you will see that there is plenty of food for everyone. You will begin to have more respect for life on the planet as it is. And not feel the need to over populate, believing you are somehow limiting the availability of human life if you do not, thinking you create life, which you do not.

You will see that you are the custodians of that opportunity to embody, but you do not have to say, "Ten children equals more people having the opportunity to be alive." Ten people just mean more people on the physical planet at one time. If you have two or three children, or four or five, - whatever you would like - one or none, if you do it with love, with compassion, then the opportunity for quality is present. I know that is not your question, but we thought we would add that. You are moving in that direction.

Your society moves more now toward limited expansion of human population. Other cultures will do the same. You will also begin to find that as you harmonize with the planet, you do not have to be caught up in the great structures of incredible density that you call cities. You will begin to spread out upon the planet in harmony and investigate the power to live closely with nature. What a wonderful time that will be. And your electronics; your technologies will serve you in that way. And as distant as you want to be, you will be as close as you have ever been, in the sense of communication.

It will allow a much finer lifestyle.

It is available to you now, of course. Nature is always present, but most people like to insulate themselves in the cities so they do not have to feel the city while they are in it. A little funny, don't you think?

We moved considerably beyond your question, but consider that there is no one truly alien or you are all alien. There are those who visit. There are those who lend their assistance. They are likened unto angels at times, in certain aspects of your scripture. Did you ever think about that? "A wheel within a wheel, within a wheel." You read Ezekiel if you want. It has been going on a long time.

*I am in a period of transition. I am hanging on very tightly and having great fears that I am not going to make it through. Do you have any suggestions on how to let go?*

Understand that the fear is born in the "monkey mind," the ego mind, which has resistance to change. It has long held the pre-eminent responsibility of creating separation, creating lack of alignment with your inner being. That is the job it has in life. So it continues to work very hard at creating patterns of fear which are also caught in the resistance to change. But you will begin to recognize that in the long run you are finding more freedom, though it does not seem that way at first, and freedom is part of the mentality of the Spirit. It is freedom to seek out and do and be what you want without false limitations.

It will gently blossom. When you feel exhausted with holding on with the ego and confident enough of the Spiritual side of yourself to begin to let go with greater ease, it will blossom.

# Meditation

*Sit in a moment of meditation.*

*Feel the energy in the room.*
*The light that is present.*
*Feel the healing,*
*the love within you.*

*May all those things*
*that you deeply desire*
*manifest now*
*and in the days to come.*

*May you more quickly attain*
*the levels of your own consciousness*
*that reveal the light of truth within you,*
*within others.*

*May you touch the hem of the garment*
*of your own awakening,*
*that joy may be present.*

*Hold these thoughts gently*
*for a moment.*

*Good evening.*

*God bless you.*

# Chapter 10

# Dreams 1 –
# Intuition And Transformation

*It is our joy that we might share with you.*

*You have been seeking to understand
the deeper aspects of your own consciousness
and have been endeavoring to uncover
the indwelling Spirit and beauty you contain.*

*It may seem to be an impossible journey at times
and at other times perhaps you feel it is so simple,
nothing could be easier.*

*I would venture to say
that you would find most of the time,
between those points of extreme,
that you are very open
to sharing your process with one another
and looking honestly within yourself.*

*At other times,
perhaps if you get too close
to issues or points of resistance
that you would not change so readily,
you shy away.*

*Not wanting to look.
Not wanting to see.*

*In those areas of your greatest discomfort,*
*you will find the dream state*
*flowing in to help reveal*
*areas of your own process*
*that can be brought forward*
*into consciousness.*

*And therefore clarified,*
*in order that you can drop*
*the fears,*
*the doubts,*
*the guilts,*
*the negative levels of consciousness.*

*And begin to appreciate who you are.*
*Who you are truly in your being.*

It is that process of unfolding that serves you in your awakened state through the dream state. A broader question might be, which is the greater reality? Are you more in touch with truth in the sleep state, or in the awakened state? Think about that a bit. It is not, of course, that you should spend your whole life sleeping - there would be little purpose to come in the body if you did that. But the body does not have free access to the Spirit under normal conditions.

While you are sleeping you are often residing in the Spiritual dimension, and the pattern of your involvement at that point in time may be brought back to your consciousness through psychological patterns. The subconscious memory is used as the vehicle for communication. Then you have the language of the Soul, which is beyond words and beyond form, brought forward through form - through remembrance of dream experience - to express something of your own truth to you.

It is important that you recognize that the mind is the builder. On every level that is so. On the conscious level, mind is the builder. On the subconscious level it is the same. So it is important for you to see where your interests and activities lead you. On what do you allow the flavor of your thoughts to be focused? Are you reading the newspapers all the time? Are you watching television? Are you giving yourself then, a steady dose of what might be termed "poison?" It is not truly poison, but it is not fulfilling in the extreme.

That is not to say you have to walk around being ignorant of the many facets of your society and what is going on in the world. You may definitely want to know about those things. But if you get immersed in the cantankerousness of outer life and lost in the seeming irresolvable difficulties between cities, between individuals, between countries, between this brand of politics and

127

another, between self and others, you will think the world has no solution - that life has little or no meaning. You will probably find your dream state reflecting that idea, since the dream state may act as a mirror to your daily consciousness, unfolding in dramatic forms, to give you that which you desire to have.

If you want the experience of separateness carried to the extreme that you believe that the world is not functioning, that there is no Spiritual reality, your dream state may approach you with that thought and say, "Okay, that is the game you want to play, we will play the game that there is no Spiritual reality." And you can dream about many different points of view or difficult processes until you are tired of it. That is one way the dream state may work.

It is like the kid in the candy store. How much candy can you eat until you get sick? You think the candy is good. It tastes good. It is exciting - as your news media is exciting. It is wonderful. But you finally get sick of too much candy, too much news media. So you change your track a bit. You start to look for that which truly nourishes. In doing so, you begin to see that there are solutions. There are patterns of evolvement. There is a deeper process in humanity that is unfolding all the time that allows mankind to move collectively forward. Even though it may look as though you are doing the two-step dance - two steps forward, one step back. But the overall process is a forward movement. That is the path that humanity works through.

In that state your psychological balance improves and your Spiritual awakening is more readily available. You begin to sense that, "Yes, I can see the light at the end of the tunnel. I do want to make a difference in my own process. I will use the tools, actively seeking out alternative levels of consciousness through the dream state, that I may explore and learn from."

In that insight, you have given yourself the real gift, because then you begin to acknowledge the guidance and counsel from the Spirit that may come. You begin to see the intermingling of your daily thoughts with your deeper desires. You begin to see how your psychic sensitivity may be brought forward so that you can analyze dream states that may be preconscious of events before they take place. That you may have prophecy or that you may begin to sense the inner workings of another and the difficulties they move through. Indeed, you may find yourself giving counsel out of your normal consciousness, which you would call the awakened state.

All of this may be seen as a psychological aspect of your own reality - as a projection of your own process - using others as examples of what you are in your multi-faceted nature. That can be an accurate description of the dream language; a way of seeing that which is part of your process, understanding the dream in an analysis of, "All this is me. If I am counseling another person in the dream state, is it a true sense that I am counseling them on some other level of their consciousness? Or am I counseling part of myself? Should I listen to the counsel?" Both may be simultaneously true. Listen to the counsel given to another in your dreams. If it is good, it is also that which you may receive for yourself.

So entertain simultaneously those seemingly opposite viewpoints. If you take them deep enough you realize that you are not separate from anyone else. Everyone is you and you belong - in a sense - to everyone else. So there is no true separation between the strictly psychological insight gained by thinking, "This is all me," and the more radical and perhaps to some, simplistic view, that the dream is literally what it says it is. That if you are talking to your cousin, giving advice in the dream, that you have done so. Both are aspects of truth and need to be considered as such.

The pattern of your own awakening will be quickened or lessened depending on your basic desire. Do you wish to move forward in time and space, as you sense it, to a greater state of awakening? Or are you happy to reside in the relative levels of frustration in which you walk? That is a key question, a critical reference point. What is your basic desire toward growth? If it is strong, then how many levels of self are you willing to be "working" on simultaneously? And we use the word "working" with quotations, because if you think it is work, it will be. You can certainly have your desire. If you desire that your Spiritual progression be hard work, then it will be hard work. But if you think, "I would rather play with my Spiritual progress and awaken the child within to more open-heartedness," then the work will be simple. Though it may at times appear frustrating and difficult. That is often the most powerful process you can utilize.

Truth, in its essence, is simple. I would repeat that. There is nothing difficult about truth. In its essence, it is simple. It is only the complexity of the outer mind desiring to have it both ways - to not want to let go of anything and to embrace everything at the same time - that makes it seem complicated. There is much that you might need to let go of in terms of your selfishness, your attitudes toward life, your lack of sensitivity to others, your lack of sensitivity to the true nature of your own being. Those are things that will drop. You will become more sensitive. You will begin to know how it feels to be another person in your extended sensitivity, and you will sense something of their beauty, something of their pain. You will have then, more compassion.

You will find that playing with the process is allowing enlightenment - letting yourself lighten up. What is light? What does the word mean? It has many meanings. Light in weight. Light in visual energy - as that which illumines and allows you to see. Light in the sense of light-hearted - perhaps happy-go-lucky. So think about where you are hard-hearted toward yourself or others, where your judgment becomes closed when your view of life is rigid and not flexible. Those are points you will find you have to let go of in order to function freely.

Freedom is a state of consciousness, not a place to which you will come. You will not see any signpost saying, "Fifteen more miles and you get to freedom! [laughter] Half an hour on the bus!" Freedom will be very much that which you, on a day-to-day basis, allow in varying degrees. At times you may feel relatively free, and then in a moment you receive some news or another person attaches their negative attitude to your thought. If you buy into it, if you absorb and accept it, then you will feel your freedom slipping away. Does that mean you should be afraid of other people's negative attitudes? Of course not. It means simply to be clear within yourself and watch your own levels of sensitivity as a barometer.

Sensitivity is wonderful when it is rightly extended to include others, to achieve deeper levels of compassion. When you feel overwhelmed by sensitivity, seek to allow the body and the personality a better balance. How is the body? Is it functioning well? Is it receiving nourishment that is natural and harmonious to your needs? Is it receiving not only the mental nourishment of what you take in daily in the way of your media and such, but also the physical nourishment of food and the emotional nourishment of dealing with others with a bit of give and take, sharing, companionship, friendship? Those are all important aspects.

What is your relationship with the planet? Have you made friends with Gaia, Mother Earth, the Earth Goddess, or whatever terms you would use? Have you made friends with that deeper portion of yourself that is the earth? Have you touched the mountains, the stars, the trees, the waters? Do you breath the air around you, delighting in its purity? Or are you choking in the pollution of the

131

cities, feeling limited and not allowing yourself to reach out and embrace because you do not feel anything worthy of embracing? That is the process. Seek out nature. Even the smallest corner of the yard or garden may reveal to you an aspect of nature that is a door to consciousness.

So let the dream state encompass all levels of your process and see it as a very active mirror. And at times see it as a guide, a vehicle through which you may achieve growth and insight. If you are faced with a difficult problem, meditate before sleeping and ask that you might receive some clarity of insight. Recognize however, that your problem may not necessarily be dealt with in the way you might expect.

Sometimes people have a limited agenda of how the problem can be solved: "How am I going to make $49,000 in the next three months?" That is a very limited agenda. "How may I have more clarity on what is important in life?" is a much broader agenda with a specific focus. You may, in the middle of your dream state, awaken and feel clarity. Perhaps the dream itself brings it, or perhaps you receive a sense of someone else's process that you have been judging harshly. The dream state allows an extended view of their insight, their worthiness, to be revealed in your thinking as a beautiful being.

Dropping old fears and doubts, or being confronted with them in a very dramatic way, may help you see some of the old patterns of thought you still hold on to that serve you no longer. The dream state in its drama, in its realism, in its simplicity can reveal much clarity. Then the issue is how to bring it into the conscious mind.

Do you wake up remembering what you have dreamed or do you go to sleep again, letting it slide away, knowing that somewhere in the middle of the night you had an insight, yet you do not know what in the world it was? What is your feeling state when you awaken in the morning? Are you still wrestling with problems? Are you still caught in some dilemma of the previous day or week? Or are you feeling refreshed as the new day greets you? Is there a sense of awakening, of gratitude, of joy as you greet the day? Do you recognize the Divine abundance, the process of Divinity around you? Do you greet the Divine in all things in a very simple way?

What is the relationship with that energy you term God? Is it an open one? Do you allow it to be simple, childlike? If so, you have received an abundance of beautiful energy. Are you quick to respond to the guidance you feel on a day-to-day basis in the conscious state, or through the dreams? Do you enact those processes upon which you have received guidance?

If you see with insight, generally that insight will prompt you to do something with it. It may be as simple as calling someone on the phone. It may be the complexity of doing some planning, some work that has been held off, which you have been a little afraid to tackle. It may simply be addressing the issues of your own perspective on what is important. What do you want to do? What gives you the greatest joy? Where do you feel blocked and limited? What situations do you feel are stuck in your life? What can be changed?

You do not need to change just for the sake of change. Some change may necessitate a lot of patience, to allow you to move through the process you are working with and enjoy the process, even if you do not always like it. It is a difficult thing, but worthy of practice. Then the dream states - as a step-by-step process - will show you, as you move along your own growth cycle, where you are going. It will show you what has been before and what is to come.

The patterns of dream awareness run deep. As we have said, they basically stem from your inner desire, which will always come up to prompt you. If your inner desire is for awakening, for Spiritual clarity, for joy and sharing energy with others in a healing and compassionate form, the dream state may become one of your greatest teachers - one of the greatest avenues of awakening for you. Inwardly expressed, yet outwardly available to put into life's experiences and your relationships with others, not just turned inward.

The dream-state can be a wonderful mine of golden energy that you continue to mine. The vein does not run out. It may get thin and then broader. You may feel richness with it at times and it may feel relatively dry at times, but it will not fail you. It is an avenue of your deeper choice made more present to the conscious mind. Seek it as such and so it will be.

Think on these things in their simplicity. See how you feel in your dream process. Notice how the body feels. Do you allow the right energy for sleep? Or is there caffeine or alcohol or nicotine heavily charging the body with something other than its natural function? Is there much worry before you sleep? Do something before you sleep to shift your mental attitude. Engage in a bit of meditation or prayer or reading or listening to music - something inspirational to change the energy pattern before you sleep.

Do you wake up to the jangle of an alarm, the sound of loud music, knocking on the door, or a ringing phone? Or do you mentally set your inner alarm so that you may awaken ten or twenty minutes earlier than you would normally and give yourself time to enjoy the richness of the harvest of the dreams? Do you have anyone as a friend, as a buddy, who is a dream-sharer? Is there such in your life? Do you have discipline to focus on the writing of dreams and keeping a journal? You can even use modern technology and make a recording, but then you are involved with another step to get it on paper.

There are tricks to remembrance that you may need to try if you do not remember. But most of all, what is your desire? What does the dream state hold for you? Is it something vital and interesting and exciting? Or is it something somebody else has talked about and you feel is a bit boring and dull? It will reflect what you think it to be. Give it a chance experimentally, and it will give you an experimental pat on the back which is always nice to receive.

We will look now at your questions.

*When I wake up I cannot grasp what I just dreamt. Is there a technique for pulling that in?*

Well, first of all, as we have suggested, do you have the time to do this? Are you laying next to someone you are afraid you are going to awaken? If you have no such fear, you may try various possibilities. One is simply to analyze how you are feeling. Do not try to find the dream. Just look at the feeling energy you have. Upon awakening, how are you feeling? If there is the tail end, or the slightest little corner of the dream state that comes in, begin to think about that. That is one aspect you may call a technique.

If you have paper and pencil there, you may try to write down the feeling state and the little corner that you have, and it may bring some back. You may find it helps to leave the body in relatively the same position you have been sleeping in. Do not change your physical position very much.

You may find you have to resort - as some do - to the utilization of a tape recorder so that you can be half asleep, half awake. Try to speak into the tape recorder with a little switch on the microphone

135

or whatever it takes to make it so simple you do not have to do anything to prepare. You can do that while remaining in the light state of sleep when you are almost awake. Try to catch what you can that way. The only problem with that is that it should be listened to later in the same day and brought forward into focus to see what it triggers. If you wait two or three days you may have very well lost the seeds waiting to be planted and they have not had then, the chance to sprout.

Another technique would be simply to say, prior to sleep, "I will remember my dreams or at least the portion thereof that is important." Ask your own teachers for assistance to do just that. Make a very real bargain with yourself and then let it go. Sometimes if you make a bargain too strongly that you will remember your dreams, you are exerting your ego-will too much and that gets in the way of the process that you want to unfold. Sometimes it is setting the wheels in motion and then letting them go, not thinking or worrying about it. You can make it such an object of focus to remember your dreams that you get in the way of the dreams. So it is a light touch. It is an artistic process, rather than a rigid discipline.

The other thing that might be of assistance is to read some very fine literature about dream work that others have experienced, to trigger the mind's activity level, its level of interest, its level of desire. That may assist you, because as those patterns become more and more familiar to the psychological awareness you have, your subconscious patterns begin to carry thoughts that dreaming is good, that basically it is helpful, it is healing. You have no fear, then, of what the dreams may bring. Then they come more easily. Sometimes there is the outer desire that you would remember your dreams, yet inwardly there is fear of what the dreams would reveal. If you have the inner fear, you block much memory.

136

Most of all, what is happening in your body when you go to sleep? Are you physically exhausted? Have you burned the candle, figuratively speaking, at both ends? Or do you go to sleep relatively blessed in your physical body, so that you are not restless, so you can move into a fine state of sleep and wake up feeling refreshed?

Those are all issues which have bearing on the memory process. Work with those things. Perhaps talk with someone about their experience. A little sharing of energy may hit a key they have found.

There is another thought with which you might alleviate some of your fear. In the early morning, before you rush off to the busyness of your day, after you have awakened and perhaps have had a bite to eat and feel truly awakened, take five to fifteen of your minutes to sit down and meditate. Go back into the feeling state when you awoke, or any part of the dream that you had when you awoke. Go back into it with a meditative focus and see what comes from that.

You may find that you are half dreaming, half meditating. Let that go, if you want. See what that brings. The dream can change through the meditation. Meditation may bring a new level of insight and ease - not a difficulty, but an ease in the process.

*I have a fear, or reluctance, to experience the dream state. Sometimes I feel separate, as if there were a veil between myself and what is being brought through in the dream state. When I meditate after I sleep, the veil is not there.*

I think you have established a pattern whereby you feel the freedom to go deeper in meditation. You have largely eliminated the fear elements that some may have concerning meditation, is that not so?

137

*Yes, that is true.*

As a meditative focus you probably sense that it is okay to go into a higher level of consciousness - that does not bother you. As you establish those patterns, it is easy to think it is okay to go high in consciousness and say, "I don't want to deal with the mess of my subconscious patterns." That may be the fear you approach in the dream state.

It is important to begin to realize that the dream state has many levels or different strata of consciousness. Some of which will approximate the reality of meditation, or even more strongly, out-of-the-body mystical levels of insight. At times the dream state will touch the level of subconscious patterning.

What would be a welcome thought - which you will have to analyze and work with a bit - is that whatever comes forth, the dream state is in its essence a gentle self-discovery. And though in dramatic form it may bring up issues you do not want to face - it is often dramatic to get your attention - it is still in its essence, a joy. It is part of the adventure and the amazing discovery process of self, and therefore worthy of respect and a certain sense of acknowledgement that, "This is okay. It is basically good. I am going to enjoy the dream state, as well as the meditative state."

That may take time to implement. It may be something you need to do a little more work with in self-analysis, so that you may approach some of those patterns of self in ways other than dreams - ways that you may feel fearful to touch. You will find that rather than a diseased portion of the body that you might have thought would fall off if you touch it, that by touching it there is an old bandage that falls off to reveal something perfectly healed.

Ask the gentle touch of your own teachers to enhance the dream

138

state. To shift it into two or three new levels of consciousness, so you may appreciate it in its variety as an objective sense of fun - an adventure of levels of self-discovery available to you. Then I think you can enjoy it.

*Sometimes there are incredible messages in dreams, but I don't understand them. How can I understand dreams more?*

You can read about it. You can work with your own and other people's dreams. You can go to classes. You can get more focused on varieties of ways to interpret. You can do workshops. Maintain an overall feeling that there is something rich to harvest and there are many tools which can be used to bring the harvest in. I think further exploration would be good.

Simply look at the dream as a meditative focus. Go deep into the meditation. If you remember your dream and you do not have a clue as to what it means, take the dream into meditation as you would other things. Take it into meditation and ask for insight about the dream - see what comes. Sometimes it can be quite succinct and very simple and to the point and the essence of the dream is revealed, though it may not give you all of the technical details as to why that essence was arrived at.

It would be like asking the computer for a summation or tally of something very complex, and in a moment's time, the computer gives you the results. That would be like the meditation. Then, in trying to analyze how the results were arrived at, the patient kind of detailed analysis of dreams that you may or may not have access to comes, depending on whether you are a computer expert! [laughter] I tease you a little bit.

Some people do not want to know at all how the computer works. They just want to know that it works. Others are quite delighted to

139

learn all the intricacies of the process. Either way, the ultimate results that you can arrive at are of great value.

*How do you distinguish between what is a memory of a dream and what is a memory of an out-of-the-body experience?*

Did you pinch yourself in the dream? I tease you a bit. I think it would be more the sense of how real it felt. The out-of-the-body level may be remembered through that which you would call normal sleep and be a close cousin to the dream state, but it takes on the depth or the quality of realness.

There is a gradual shedding border between lucid dreaming or very clear states of dream awareness, and those things which you might term out-of-the-body experiences. There are many doors, and you could say that you are looking through two doors that are open at the same time. That may be the gradation area you are working with and wondering which door to appreciate the most.

Ultimately it does not matter what title you put on it. What do you derive from it? Does it give inspiration? Does it give insight? Does it allow you to love yourself and others more deeply? That is what is important.

*I've been frustrated in my dream work. I can interpret other's dreams, but have problems with my own. I have a recurring dream. This same thing keeps coming back at me. I guess the best thing to do would be to get some help from other people.*

It might be also that you look at the dream and what process it is dealing with. It is one thing to have an intellectual insight, it is something else to have a feeling, emotional insight. For example, if you are dealing with a fear that stems from childhood, that may also have been a pattern of energy that your parents entertained.

140

That may be deeply ingrained and you may have a dream that clearly reveals its presence and suggests to you that this is a very strong pattern that you need to move through. You recognize it as such, you have clear insight into the psychological origins, you understand how it came to be, you are anxious to have it removed in the sense of having it clarified, and yet the same pattern re-exerts itself in different forms. That indicates that you have not yet achieved that point of deep integration of self that would let it dissolve. It is not saying you do not understand it. It is simply saying you have not achieved the point of release.

Assistance from others may also assist you in the release, but it may not lend any new insight into why it is there and what it is. It is simply the point of letting go, of finalizing the focus through the energy that you term compassion and wisdom and letting that dissolve what is at issue.

*Does controlling or changing the outcome of the dream take away from the learning process?*

Controlling to the level of lucid dreaming? When you are dreaming and you are aware that you are dreaming, and therefore the dream is the plaything of your daily consciousness to some extent? What do you want to know? Is it valuable, and if so, why?

*Yes.*

I understand your question. What you are trying to say is - are you receiving the proper learning? Is there a deeper message to the dream that you may be compromising? What is the deeper finality? Is there a gift, or grace that comes to you in the dream that you are not allowing to fulfill itself? Or is it truly a sense of learning that you create your own reality and is another aspect of seeing how consciousness can be shifted?

141

It can be either of those or both, or neither. How is that for complication! More importantly, do you receive joy from it? For example, sexuality is a big issue in the dream state and some would say, "Oh, I want to create a dream of sleeping with so and so." Then they would think they are fulfilling their deeper nature, when in truth they might have a much broader experience of greater joy, greater richness in the energy, if they would allow the dream to fulfill itself. They would receive a deeper sense of true heart opening, a deeper sense of love. What you are wondering about is if the ego gets in the way by confronting the process with its own desires. Sometimes that may be very much what happens.

It is important to look at the psychological needs of the person who is experiencing the dream as an outgrowth of fulfillment for those needs. Or, if you look at the possibility of moving to a place where you realize you are dreaming. And you want to creatively challenge a sense of frustration or a sense of limitation - a sense of being victimized as the dream-state often brings forward. Then you are exerting your capacity for change, your capacity to create, and you are utilizing some Spiritual muscles that are very good to exercise.

It is a step. The important thing would be, what is the basic energy? How much compassion is present? That is always a question you can level at any experience, on any level of your being; how much compassion is present? If there is compassion present, no problem. That state of what might be termed lucid dreaming is a doorway through which you may go to recognize that you are a free agent in the universe. You can travel. You can be with those of similar vibration. You can talk with others. You can study and learn. You can teach. You can share. Any number of possibilities present themselves to you on a deeper level of your consciousness which is naturally present. You are doing this much more than you realize. You normally don not have a memory of it.

142

The clear state of lucid dreaming, may be a door through which you begin to experience the dimension that sometimes has been called out-of-the-body. Out of your physical body would be a better term, since there is never a time you do not have a body. You always have a body, though it may not be a physical one.

Pray about it. Seek your own guidance on the specific details where you run into that. See what compassion brings you. Remember, also, dreams can be fun! Everybody gets so serious sometimes at the weighty prospect of delving into the subconscious mind. Think of the delight that children exhibit in life. Their dreams often have the same energy. If their outer circumstances are not heavily weighted by negative emotional energy of others, children have delightful dreams and a delightful life process which might be a model or a guide to allowing yourself such freedom of expression.

*When we go into the subconscious, is that like going deeper into the Spirit?*

Well, in the ultimate sense yes, in that as you go deeper into your being you are deepening your contact with the Spirit. In traditional terminology though, the subconscious mind is sometimes seen to be the barrier between your ordinary mind and the Spirit. It is a poor analysis, but that is the way some people would think about it. The subconscious is more the memory bank, the great computer, and the storage system of memory, of feeling, of energies, not only of this life but of other lives as well.

It penetrates to that level which may assist you in seeing who you are, why you are present in the body now, what issues you have brought forward to deal with. And there may be memories present in the subconscious of deep Spiritual insight which offer additional doors to guide you through, to experience the Spirit, the true Self.

Any time you deepen your appreciation of who and what you are, ultimately you help to awaken the Spirit. It is also true though, that sometimes you look only to the subconscious patterns for investigation, and feel that is the total essence of what you are and what you have to work with, and miss a very direct approach such as meditation, such as healing, which may give you a very direct energy state.

That does not mean you will have to let go of all psychological processing. In fact it will be just the opposite. As you allow the deeper state of meditation, of healing, of altered states of consciousness to take place, you will automatically begin to open the subconscious mind to bring up that which is important to be dealt with. That with which you are ready to deal. It will be an automatic function. So they work in tandem, in balance.

The mind ultimately is one, not split into categories. But for ease of translation of interpretation, it becomes necessary to speak in the generalization of three categories: body consciousness, mental and emotional consciousness, and spiritual consciousness. Or, if you talk of the mind state - the physical, the mental, and the spiritual - relating to the physical, which is the daily consciousness, the emotional, which would be more the subconscious, and the Spiritual as super-conscious.

*Does our higher Self speak to us through dreams?*

Absolutely. Dreams may have the higher Self functioning very clearly. And at times they may also reveal your fears, which you would scarcely say is your higher Self. Yet those two are there to be looked at and brought forward with compassion. Certainly it is important to notice that dreams vary widely in the energy that they involve in your life. You would not necessarily place equal attention on all dreams, but they all have value.

144

For example, if you are in a school situation in your physical life and there are final exams coming. And you have a dream that you begin to go through a door to take a final examination and you feel, "No, I should not take that final exam." And then you wake up and think, "My dream said I should not take that exam." Which is the true interpretation: That you should not take the final exam? Or that your fear about the upcoming test is simply being objectified and you need to move through the fear and not let it limit you? That would be an example of a subconscious pattern.

You may have a super-conscious aspect of the dream state that simply says, "Don't take this test because this is not the examination of energy you wish to look at." It may be that there is an alternative. For example, you may be able to do a project, a research process. Or it may be simply that the field that the test serves as an examination entrance into represents something you do not want to do in life. How would you tell the difference? It seems a little tricky, doesn't it? It would be a deeper state of knowing; what is the fear, what is the joy. I hope this example serves you to cause some delineation or some definition in your thinking about how to respond to the dream energy.

Some dreams may carry a very direct message. For example, there is an opportunity coming and you dream of somebody knocking on a door and giving you a form to fill out as though you were receiving a package. You fill out the form and they quickly do a calculation to see if you are the right person, and lo and behold, you have won something of great value. That dream comes to you and you think about it in the morning and the days following and wonder, what does it mean?

Finally, what it does deal with is that someone calls you on the phone and they are asking you to take over the responsibility of a certain project that they do not have time for. It may be something involving a bit of free time on your part, something donated, perhaps there is no money involved. Part of your mind takes issue, saying, "Oh, I am so busy, I don't have time for another volunteer job which will require my energy." And yet the deeper Self is saying, "Go ahead and do it," knowing, as it does, that behind the process of this particular job there is the possibility, very strongly present, of meeting someone you should meet. So through that activity you come into the acquaintance, the friendship of someone that you have been longing to meet. And that is what the dream was portraying, "Here is a gift." Yet it did not look like a gift when it was presented to you in the physical life. It looked like another responsibility that you were tempted not to take on because you felt overburdened. At that point it would be then, of interest to check inside: "Should I take this one or not?"

I think we should not hold the body any longer. It has been our joy to be present with you.

# Meditation

*If you would like,*
*hold a moment of meditation.*

*Go within and ask the presence of the higher Self*
*to help reveal to you your own inner clarity.*

*Revealing all of life's process,*
*but more particularly this time,*
*that which has to do with the dream state,*
*with the meditative qualities,*
*the insightful qualities of the dream state.*

*Go within now and look at a dream.*
*Bring a dream back that you have had recently.*

*Look at it in the meditation.*
*Ask for insight of that dream.*

*Ask that a gift may be given to you from the higher Self.*
*Take the gift,*
*beautifully wrapped,*
*and begin to open it.*
*Embrace the gift in your wisdom and your love.*

*Know that you are deeply loved in all things*
*by that Universal energy which penetrates your life*
*at every turning in the path.*

*You may find reflected back to you*
*a sense of joy of the universe,*
*if you will so allow it.*

147

*May it be so for each of you.*

*Good evening*
*and God bless you.*

# Chapter 11

# Dreams 2 –
# Intuition And Transformation

*God bless you.*
*It is our joy that we might share with you.*

*You have been seeking to witness*
*within your own heart*
*that greater joy of life*
*and to find ways to bring it into sharper focus.*

*To more clearly allow*
*the truth of your own perspective to be strong.*
*And to find your love for others deepening.*

*You have been seeking to discover*
*that which no longer serves you.*
*So you can drop it,*
*and draw that which does serve you closer.*

*So you begin to truly embark*
*on that threshold of awakening consciousness,*
*and that touch-in with the Divine*
*under all circumstances.*

You are not limited to the outer mind's reference, which at times is severely limited. At other times it may be broader. It is well that you might recognize the on-goingness of your consciousness at all levels of your being. There is the dream state, through sleep, which is one of the major barriers to conscious understanding if it is not seen as worthy. Some would say, "It is totally unimportant; it has no value," and then in neglecting that value, they find there are missing elements in their awakening.

That is not to say that you must understand dreams to be awakened. It is rather to suggest that on a deeper level, your physical experience of life may also be seen as a dream. Think about that. The comparison may be well put if you think about how, in your ordinary dreams, you have one level of reality and in your ordinary waking life you have another level of reality, but that, in a sense, is also a dream. And in the greater state of your awakening you move out of dream consciousness - the night dream and the day dream - and you move into an awakened state.

You do not necessarily have to go through the night dream to the day dream to the awakened state. You can go directly - anytime - to an awakened state if you will allow it. It is not too much to say that you are in your Divine heritage now. Perhaps not as fully as you would like, but glimpses of it are seen by you, nonetheless, and you may find extremely high levels of consciousness flowing through you at times. So do not neglect to witness the beauty that is there, regardless of whatever else is going on.

The dream state then becomes an aspect of consciousness which may reflect joy. It may bring deeper wisdom to you. It may begin to penetrate through the old-fashioned view, which is an age-old untruth, that you are limited to your body - that you are limited to a single level of consciousness. You are not so limited. You are not limited to the physical body as your only receptacle of

150

consciousness. You are multi-dimensional in your being. You have many levels of consciousness and the physical dimension is one that is very important. But it is not enough to say, "I am just a physical being." You are not just a physical being. You are much more.

You are a child of the Divine. You are an awakened being, moving toward greater awakening and those levels of consciousness you have yet to explore. Those levels of consciousness know you fully, though you may not know them. In retrospect you will see that you have always known, in the higher levels of your consciousness, all the lesser levels. Each phase of consciousness awakening opens to include all that has gone before. And it finally opens to include a state called timelessness. There was never a time when you were not Divinely aware, except at the level of the conscious mind.

So the dreams flowing as they do, from deeper levels of reality, allow you to penetrate the inner awakening. Not all dreams, of course, have that caliber, but some do. Some will remind you of what and who you are. Other dreams may remind you of what you are working on - the difficulties you are developing to form lessons that you are working with to explore and grow. Some dreams will deeply remind you of your essence, if you will allow it, and the experience of such dreams goes far beyond the level of energy normally associated with dreaming.

The experience of those extended states of consciousness may move you to the deeper awareness where you realize you are not limited to your physical body. You may travel in this vast universe, out of the body. You call it out of the physical body, but you always have a body. I want to emphasize that. You always have a body and it is perfectly right for the level of consciousness you wish to explore. You cannot take your physical body with you - perhaps a few have - but I do not think most of you will find that expedient or even necessary when you leave the body.

151

You will recognize that you have been a Spirit, and that in your Spirit being, you have done many things, related accordingly to what you want to do. That which you desire is your level of manifestation. If you desire the highest level, the manifestation you will experience will be very high. In the process of your high states you may have certain awakened feelings of being beyond the body - not limited to it, but being beyond it. It is wonderful to know that you can experience what you deeply desire to experience. If your desire is deep, the heavens will open.

Think of your deep desire to grow and expand in the material kingdom and in the Spiritual kingdom. The two are not separated - they have an inter-connection. They are, in a sense, synonymous with your overall process of awakening. Since you have a physical vehicle you call the body, use it in wisdom. Use it in joy. Let it be part of the growth and development you want to achieve. Let it be a vehicle for your Soul consciousness, for your deeper consciousness. Do not be hesitant to share with one another. If someone is in the dream state with you, share with them. Perhaps they might remember, and in so doing, will help you see beyond the level of physical interpretation you normally call dreams.

You may begin to see something of the Spirit, telepathy, precognition, and different issues being brought into greater focus, so that you will understand the other person more clearly. The dream state is not limited. It has vast potential. You can penetrate into the future. You can move into the past. You can deal with timelessness. You can ascertain what it is to be a gifted instrument of the Spirit, with various levels and forms and shapes of energy moving through you. You can even create. If you want to be involved in creative writing for example, you may find you write something very beautiful in the Spirit. It may be difficult to remember just what you have written, but at least it will give you the impetus to try.

152

You would be surprised how many times the Spirit has come to visit you and the only response you can make to the outer mind is through the dream state. You have a dream, perhaps, of a cousin coming, or an uncle coming into your household that you want to share with, someone you have had little chance to communicate with. So you take the chance to communicate with this uncle and you begin to sense that it may not be an uncle at all. It may be someone who was gifted to act as a channel, and desired to speak with you and so took this "short cut."

In other words, someone may come to you in the Spirit simply as an aspect of your own dreaming - you remember it in the conscious mind, and yet the reality that prompted it was larger than just your own internal process. It was a greater experience.

Someone in the body that you know, physically, or that you are going to know, or that you might have known in the past, may come to you in that altered state of consciousness you would call dreaming, but it is much more than a dream. You may have a deep conversation - a deep sharing. You may do some healing. You may do some work together. You may engage in all kinds of creative endeavors. And you may remember it, and they may not. It may come forth in your conscious mind as just a dream, but on a deeper level you will remember. Sometimes you may be able to share the experience that you call dreaming and recognize it as more than a dream.

Those are ways to allow the mind to begin to witness its own greater beauty, its own greater dimensionality. You might begin to size up, and feel for yourself that your life - your experience of life - is due to your own choice, your own growth, your own needs that are to be met and that are being met. You might begin to take responsibility for creating whatever it is you want to create.

It would not hurt to start thinking about dreams as an unlimited resource that will often give you pieces of the puzzle that are missing in the outer life. Think of them as a way to explore more deeply; a way to see what healing is about, a way to feel what it is to be clairvoyant, a way to understand the depth of another's process or problem, and be able to assist them.

There are many ways to channel energy. Most important is that you keep a sense of charity, a sense of humility. Not in the ordinary sense, but in the sense of beauty - the sense of humility that comes to you when you witness great beauty. If you keep that sense, I think you will find that you can communicate to others very easily what you can do.

*I have learned about "turning the dream around." For example, in one dream there is a lion. In the dream I decided to tame it. When I did that, the whole dream spun around and the fear changed.*

I think what you are experiencing is a reflection of how Divine law works on a deeper level. When you meet and confront your fears and do something to change the energy, your experience of reality shifts. That is true in waking life, as you have found it to be in the dream. So it is a very fine and sound psychological process to be able to confront fear and to deal and work with it. The dream state may be symbolic of that process, since that is what you are essentially doing. I do not want to tell you that every dream has to be a confrontation with fear - it certainly does not. But if there is something you have fear of in a dream, and you deal with it, you are effectively learning how to strengthen your own consciousness.

*I do not dream. I think the reason is that as a child I suffered a tremendous amount of fear which resulted in a lot of nightmares.*

You had headaches too, didn't you?

154

*Yes. When I left my family I started having astral experiences. I was always flying in my dreams. How do you distinguish a dream from an astral experience? Later, when I became involved in a career, I did a lot of daydreaming, and was told I was mentally preoccupied, yet this was when I did my best creative work.*

Well, I think you simply have allowed yourself to bring the effect of dreaming to the conscious mind, through what you term daydreams. You do not have to have classically described dreams to experience the same value. For you - so you taste the various levels of consciousness which you have - the difference between the dream state and what you might term as an astral or out-of-the-body experience is often one of degree. You may remember it through the mechanism that you would consciously remember the dreams through also, but it has a more vital quality; a vibrancy about it; a certain sense of reality. It may or may not have greater meaning. You may have a very profound dream that offers tremendous insight. You may have a very ordinary out-of-the-body experience which may not necessarily offer tremendous insight.

I do not want you to think that dreams are not important if you start to do some out-of-the-body travel. Dreams may still serve you very richly, as well as out-of-the-body experiences. That is a very poor term, by the way - you are never truly out of your physical body. In any level of consciousness, the body that you have, feels physical - strange as that may sound. It is not a physical body in the sense that you have the physical body you are now sitting in, that is figurative and literal: "sitting in your body". Your body is a vehicle for consciousness to express and explore in the physical dimension. And in other dimensions you also have a body that is a vehicle which you express and explore as a soul-being in that level of energy. And it will be just as real and tangible - to that level - as the level you are in that you call the physical.

155

So dreams may resonate through all those levels and function well in each one, or they may at times feel radically different, depending on which level of consciousness you express or explore through.

*I think I have a mental block about dreaming. I seem to enjoy daydreaming, yet I cannot remember my dreams at night.*

Well, let us not call it a "mental block." Let us just say you are processing in a different way. There may come a time when you process in the ordinary dream state, but rather than choosing to think of yourself as limited in comparison to others, think about the creative work that you have just described and how you get it accomplished. In the ordinary reverie that you would call the daydream it may serve the same work, very valuably. Then you do not have the great effort to try to remember and it is much easier to remember then. So maybe you have cheated everybody else! I tease you a little. It does not matter which shaft you follow when you go after the vein of gold.

*Why do I sometimes dream in color, and other times just in black and white?*

Good question. Some people tend to dream only in black and white - others only in color. Maybe you like the oldies but goodies, as well as the new ones! [laughter] I tease you a little. It would not be fair to say that a dream in color is more important than one in black and white, but often it does indicate a deeper intensity of feeling energy. Dreaming in color may be an indication that you could put forth a little extra effort to try to work with the dream, either in written form or in your understanding. Work with it a bit.

The color may also add another dimension of clarity. It may enhance your process of interpretation, by looking at colors and their meanings, too.

The important thing to notice when you work with dreams, is that there will be certain symbols you come to accept as having a given meaning. The subconscious mind will use those symbols as a kind of vocabulary - a basic symbolism vocabulary to say what it wants to say. Your subconscious mind is there to teach; to share with you.

*I have a fear of letting go to sleep, of losing consciousness, of letting go of the ego. What is there without ego? What does it mean for us all to be one, whether it is one in the dream, or one in death? What do we have of ourselves that's left?*

You will never lose your individuality. You will gain universality. It is just a point of emphasis. Some, in exploring what it is to be awakened, would emphasis that you are totally at one; that there is no ego resident. To have no ego does not mean that you are un-individualized. The individuality you carry is unique. It has been generated through many experiences that the ego has also been part of, but the ego is not necessary to your individuality.

Your individuality may seem to have ego, but that is a level of expression. Let me draw an analogy. If you go to a movie and you see a projection of a reality on the screen, that would be similar to the ego. The ego is a projection of a reality. What is real, though, is that which was there when the film was being shot. That is the reality. So the higher Self, at the Soul level, the individuality that you contain, is there. It is solid. It is real. It is not a projection. The ego would hold the projection and think that that is real, when it is not.

*There would still be consciousness, then?*

There is always consciousness. You cannot lose consciousness. You can shift consciousness and shift points of view, points of perspective, but the beingness that you are, never loses consciousness, even through death. You cannot lose consciousness. You can explore it in new ways, you can expand it, you can lose the consciousness of the ego, which may be called the ego death. In a certain sense, any awakening process is preceded by a sense of ego death. It may be a very subtle sense, with no fear at all. It may be a very strong, dramatic experience with a lot of fear involved. But ultimately, you begin to trust that you cannot disappear. There is nothing to fear.

Meditation helps. Prayer helps. The realization of the experiences others have moved through may help. But ultimately you will work out your fear and trembling with a greater joy of the Spirit overshadowing all else. You will come to know there is nothing to fear, not even fear itself. When you do that you let go of the fear. And you will not suddenly dissolve. You will still be uniquely yourself. You will, if anything, be more yourself. There will be an expansion.

Just remember that out of fear of death comes fear of life. If you do not fear death of the ego or anything else, you will not fear the experience of life. And it comes. Do not feel like you have to throw all your fears out overnight. A more practical way to work on it is to love more. Love dissolves fear in every area where fear may exist. Great love, great compassion dissolves it.

The only real fear is the lack of understanding of what love is. I do not mean intellectual understanding. I mean the knowingness that love brings. Without it, fear resides. With it, fear cannot reside in any category of thinking, whether it be subconscious patterns, childhood patterns, sleeping patterns, awakened patterns, fear of expressing yourself to others, fear of being who you really are, or

158

fear of letting go of tight control.

The greatest control is to know you do not need any. Some people experience fear associated with some form of psychic protection, when the true Self knows nothing can harm you, nothing can touch you. You are individualized. You are unique. You are beautiful. You are Divinity. All these things you can explore, because the drama the personality likes to express is one of exploration, one of variations in energy, one of contrasting values.

Ultimately, you are without distinction in the essence of your being, and yet you carry tremendous distinction in the essence of your individuality. So you cannot be separated from others, yet at the same time, you cannot lose your individuality. You will always be uniquely yourself.

# Meditation

*Let us take a moment*
*for you to hold a meditation.*

*Go within yourself*
*to that high point of consciousness.*

*You may figuratively sense it*
*as golden light flowing through you.*

*In your mind,*
*know that dreams are a part*
*of your deeper levels of consciousness.*

*And in your meditation*
*ask for assistance*

*Ask that there may be greater clarity*
*over the very deep level of dreaming*
*wherein the Self is revealed.*

*The mighty Self*
*of love and compassion*
*is revealed.*

*Honor the various levels*
*of your process.*

*In the body.*
*In the daily mind.*
*And in the deeper joy*
*that you feel*

*through your prayers,*
*your meditations.*

*Honor the need*
*to be in communication with others.*
*Honor the need*
*to share with others.*
*Honor the need*
*to be in communication*
*with those who guide you.*

*And finally,*
*honor that connection*
*to the higher Self.*

*And in the honoring,*
*let there be a blessing*
*of each of those aspects.*

*As a beautifully woven net of jewels*
*that you may place upon yourself*
*to move out into meeting the world.*

*Let there be a sense of self*
*that you may deeply touch and love,*
*and in times of need,*
*you will find that steady cup to drink from.*

*It has been our great joy to share with you.*
*Know that you walk not alone.*
*There are those that lend their assistance gladly,*
*for it gives them great joy to do so.*

*Good evening. God bless you.*

Chapter 12

# Love, Sexuality And Healing

*God bless you.*
*It is our joy that we might share with you.*

*It has been many years*
*that each of you finds yourself in the body.*

*Yet that time which you experience*
*in your thinking as very long*
*is rather brief in the vision of the soul.*

*For even that which might be considered*
*a lengthy embodiment;*
*eighty, ninety, one hundred,*
*or even more of your years,*
*is to the soul a very brief form of time.*

*A very brief experience*
*worthy of all due respect,*
*but not in its essence*
*the sum total of your being.*

*You are much larger,*
*much greater than you might believe.*

*And the universe bows before you.*
*Not to your ego,*
*but to your true beauty.*

*Mankind inhabits the flesh*
*to become acquainted*
*with the way of the world.*

*And to discover how that*
*which seems separated from the Divine*
*may reunite and link itself*
*again consciously with the Divine essence.*

*In truth you have never been separated.*
*You are not now separated.*
*Nor can you ever be separated*
*from the Divine essence*
*which flows through all things,*
*everywhere present.*

However, that which you hold as reality in the conscious mind, your belief about who you are, constitutes a separation. However intense you might feel about your individuality, thinking that you will lose it if you re-merge yourself with the Divine, know that that is the personality's limited view. In truth you lose nothing. You retain that which is the individual spark, that which you have created, that which you have nurtured through many embodiments, and you gain a universe in the bargain.

To reconnect with your Divine source is to find all for which you hunger. The hunger you feel may express itself in different ways. It may be the desire to express your individual uniqueness through the written word, or through some spontaneous activity of giving happiness to others. Perhaps you are a humorist on the stage of life, poking fun at those things which need to be poked fun at. That too is God.

Perhaps you work diligently to support a family, or to bring substance into physical existence for the very practical needs of self and others. Do you not then, seek harmony with nature, with your surroundings, with your environment, in such practice? Is it not an aspect of love, though you might call it "duty?" You might even call it boring. Many of you would call your work that. But it too represents the desire on your part to do something that is sustaining.

I know it may seem difficult to see Divine process in the everyday, "humdrum" reality. If you feel bored with life, do not be surprised if life, chuckling in its deeper awareness, gives you a little more to be bored with, so you can become very tired of being bored! Your Spirit can never be bored. Your deeper Self embraces the Divine chuckle. It embraces the wonderful unity that you seek to experience.

So as you look at the processes called healing, or love, or sexuality, embrace the broader wisdom of what you hunger for. If you are with one you love deeply, sexuality becomes a deepening experience, to bridge the gap between the physical, mental, emotional self, the Spirit that you are, with another. Find the spark of the Divine within them that you might share - they with you and you with them.

If sexuality is engaged in just to placate a momentary desire, it becomes rather boring, don't you think? Have you not found yourself exceedingly bored when you do not love someone deeply? The momentary awareness of pleasure may be intense, since the body has deep programming to procreate, to bring other beings into the physical dimension, but in the deeper sense of Self you have a need of expression for many levels of consciousness. This is not to deny your physical substance; your physical being, your ability to find pleasure in the body as a temple, as a vehicle for the Divine presence. One of the greater pleasures, one of the more important aspects of your existence is the linkage you make that constitutes sexuality. That is one of the deeper powers flowing through you. But it is not enough to express sexuality just for its own sake. It needs to be coupled with love.

There is a bit of a paradox, because in sexuality often the desire to be a bit possessive develops. Again, it is the instinctual awareness to perpetuate the species, to create a home nest. But on the deeper level, where love is present, where deep love is present, sexuality becomes rather universal. That is not to say that you go to bed with everyone to express your love, but in truth, as you love one deeply who is your lover, you find that it opens the door for you to see others - to see the Divine within them and know your love for them. And that love may easily be expressed in the form of words, or in some form of communication, in some form of caring and healing. You may feel that the act of healing is very different in its

166

energy flow than sexuality, but in essence they both speak of Divine presence. They both speak of a hunger and a move toward unity.

Sexuality often carries the need to be sustained in a singular relationship, so that you do not destroy the bonds of your feeling of deep love for another by being scattered in your energy. I hope you do not take this as a moralistic lesson. We are speaking of the patterns of how you might fulfill your own deeper desire.

I am confident all of you have engaged in a bit of exploration and experimentation to find what works for you personally. In that way you find your truth - not that of another. I would not have you accept the words that are spoken here and then say, "I should never be sexual with anyone unless I am deeply in love with them." Then perhaps you set up such resistance that you do not allow yourself to love. I do not want any artificial thoughts in your mind. The human race has already created enough programming around sexuality. It needs to be more deeply understood as an energy cycle. It has its source in healing, it has its source in unity. It has its source in the perpetuation of the species. Is that not important? Of course it is.

If you look at love in the human sense, it may constitute many things: love of a person, love of a place, love of a country or love of self in the ordinary sense of your ego self. All are wonderful ways to feel love. But love on other levels which more deeply express the Spirit begin to touch the core of human nature. The love is there to find ways to allow others to awaken to their beauty. The love is there to express the Spirit - both to receive and give. Love is there to be creative, to be expressive of your individual uniqueness, and yet to find the Divine presence flowing through you. Those are very strong levels of love.

The Spirit is touched by all that transpires in the physical plane, so it would be true to say there can be no expression that is not, in some sense, a reflection of the Spirit of uniqueness that you carry. The more powerful aspects of love need no words. Indeed, the words may get in the way.

There is the reciprocation of energy - the resonance of energy with another in the sense that you love them just the way they are and you do not have to change them. Of course there is room for their evolution, but your love is not predicated on standards that are rigidly structured.

To see another through the Spirit is to love them always. It may not be to like them always. I want to emphasize that possibility. If you see someone whose consciousness is devoid of much resonance of the Spirit - they come to you, perhaps, in an alcoholic stupor, or they come to you in great emotional upset - part of your mind may think, "I don't like this person, at least not in their present state of consciousness." It is okay to feel that you do not like them. But the Spirit love that you may feel can bypass or penetrate through that disguise of the outer self, and see the Divine essence so deeply present within them that nothing but love is felt. That is your deep Divinity expressing.

There is an example you have in your scripture: There was a woman caught in an act of adultery and in the time of that culture, to stone one such as her was acceptable. Of course that was done with a lot of righteous indignation; a lot of finger pointing and feelings of superiority; a lot of judgment. The man Jesus looked upon the multitudes and upon the woman and he saw her deeper need, her great desire for love of the universe, which she expressed through sexuality. She was hungering for something greater. With great compassion he also saw the limitation of the multitude gathered. Not in great anger, but in true beingness of Spirit, he

168

looked upon them - you might say looked into their consciousness - to witness to them their own iniquities, their own shortcomings, and he said, "He who is without sin cast the first stone." Consequently everyone left, since they were faced with their own reflection of ego. In the purity of his consciousness, they could not abide in that state and they left.

Perhaps you have heard that story before. It was an expression of Divine mind, an expression of deep love, both for those who might be raised to witness their own shortcomings and cease to judge others so harshly, and for the woman with whom he talked. She came, in this awareness, to be a follower because her love was recognized in its true essence, rather than that which would be easily criticized. She was seen in her purity and of course that brought healing.

Healing is touching that deep level of consciousness where the Spirit is present. And whether the illness be of the mind, the body, the Spirit; whether it be subjective or external, true healing is that linkage with the inner world - that broader window of the universe, that greater sense of love which is a deep sense of respect for self and all others. In that flow of energy, illness does not exist, for dis-ease is a sense of separation from the Divine Self.

When perfect love is present, it casts out fear. When perfect love is present, it is the essence of healing. When perfect love is present, there may be deep union with another. And perhaps it may not be a sexual union, as the flow of energy may be so intense that sexuality cannot enhance that awareness.

That does not mean that one must be non-sexual to be conscious. It simply means that there are levels of consciousness which are intensely more superior to the ordinary form of love-making.

169

Love-making is a move in the right direction. It is a move toward a sense of unity. But as the internal awareness opens, the centers, the chakras, become more deeply aligned to the planet and energy flows more quickly to that which is the heart, the crown. Then perhaps love is so intense that sexuality does not add anything. It becomes an option, not a necessity.

Rather than worrying about when you might reach such an exalted state, begin to do a bit of work with healing: prayer, meditation, perhaps time set aside to work with another, both to give and receive. This may show you much of how Divine energy feels. It may show you its resonance within you, that you are not alone on the planet, that you have guidance. In the act of bringing healing, deep is the love that is felt. Of course you do not create the love, but it flows through you and therefore translates to your awareness. It makes the difference in how you appreciate your own being, how you see others, how you may love them deeply.

The essence of healing is love. In the practice of healing comes deep peace. With that deep peace, you may find a great richness in your personal life. When love is expressed in sexual form it can be of great beauty. When love is expressed in the joy that you share with one whom you hold dear, perhaps in friendship, or in love, there is a resonance of the heart that is nurturing and energizing.

"All of these things ye may do, and even greater," was spoken long ago, meaning of course miraculous happenings within yourself. If there are changes of perspective, new doors open that allow love to be more present, and that is its own miracle. It may not be the instantaneous healing of the flesh; it may be a changing of your perspective that allows you to see yourself more deeply.

From that which is dramatic to that which is very subtle, look to see how love may enhance your life and how you may embrace it, for it dwells within you, waiting to be explored and expressed. Ask that you may understand. Ask that you may have that awareness. Ask that you may deeply love, for such is the stuff of heaven.

Perhaps we may share with you now, in those areas that may have been triggered by our discussion - those areas of your own concern for harmony and self-help. Perhaps ways you feel your own blockage, that we might examine to show you a bit more of your own light.

*What is depression and how can it be fought?*

Look at the whole consciousness: you are body, mind and Spirit. If you affect any one of those areas - which are a unit - you will affect the basis of all areas. If you experience psychic depression, an easy way to deal with it is to bring the body, physically, into a greater state of happiness. Have more playfulness. Clear the diet so it is more beneficial to the physical system. For the mind, read inspirational writings which are uplifting. Listen to music that feels positive and healthy. There are many ways you can work with those feelings that will make them transform, become transparent and go away.

Sometimes you may attack them directly, but often what that does is solidify what you think may be a problem into a full-fledged problem. Because you have invested so much energy in it, it needs to be really powerful to be worthy of that invested energy. Many times people make their problem bigger simply because they call it a problem. Often the playful approach can dislodge the thought of unworthiness.

*Can you speak about degenerative illnesses and how diet may help?*

171

Many things can help. The attitude of personal love is of great importance. We speak about diet in ways that I think step on most people's toes! First of all, in your modern civilization, you have at your disposal "instant everything." Quick this, quick that. Instant enlightenment even, these days! But there is no free lunch. You do not get anything for nothing, and so it is also with food.

If you have a quick fix of food, it may have a lot of sugar which is highly refined, and that brings you a boost of energy and then a depression. You may eat a lot of heavier meats and foods that taste good, and yet they bring a bit of depression to the body. So then of course you want a quick cup of coffee to give you a little more energy, and you leave the meal with the body in a lot of distress.

This goes on month after month, year after year, until the pancreas grows tired, the adrenal system becomes weakened, and then you begin to find you have no stamina, no basic drive of energy to sustain you. You want to keep on working very hard, playing very hard, going to a lot of parties, and drinking a lot of alcohol, yet you cannot seem to function as well as you used to. So you drink a little more coffee, to keep going even more. And the whole cycle becomes like the dog biting his tail - trying to get out of it and not knowing why it keeps going in a circle.

That is an extreme example, but let me put it very succinctly: if there is life force in the food, the body will generally thrive on it. If the food is devoid of life force, then it provides some sustenance, but it does not truly bring a sense of well-being. Much of the food you consume has no great life force in it. Simply put, cut out the refined starches, the refined sugars, the artificial stimulants, and your body is going to be a lot happier. You are going to be a lot happier. And then you do not have to worry so much about weight, either. Everybody is worried about a few extra pounds. If you take away the refined starches, the refined sugars, you will not have a

172

weight problem.

The other side of that whole process, though, is to feel happy with yourself. It is okay to make change slowly. You do not have to suddenly make a total change. Change one thing at a time.

*Could you explain what soul-mates and twin-souls are?*

In theory, the soul-mate is your other half - the beingness that you were originally in its perfection which was split into what many have termed the female and male elements. Many think they go their separate incarnational ways for many lives until they finally come back together for the most perfect and beautiful relationship. The trouble is, everyone gets the idea so caught in romanticism that they fail to appreciate that your soul-mate might not even be on the planet! Perhaps it is giving you some guidance from the Spirit. Or your soul-mate may be an old man, or an old woman, or a very young child. Perhaps you are not meant to be with that person in this life.

There are those, of course, whose affinity for you, and yours for them, would constitute a sense of soul-mate. If you are honest with somebody you have a deep affinity for, you might as well call them your soul-mate, since that deep affinity can do much to allow progression for both of you. But do not try to find the guarantee and say, "I want my soul-mate, and only that." Perhaps you would not even like your soul-mate if you met them!

On a broader basis, what does it mean to have a soul-mate? Does it not mean to unify with another in a very deep and Divine way? And are not each one of you, ultimately, complete unto yourselves? As you become conscious more deeply, you will begin to find that you can do things you had not thought you could do. You will begin to find doors that open that you did not think could

173

open. Opportunities come that you did not think possible. Ultimately you will begin to see that as you embrace your own Divinity, your love for others deepens and deepens. You might even begin to think that the human race everywhere - whether in the body or the Spirit - is your soul-mate. What a wonderful feeling that is.

Certainly in relationship, look to see how you may feel more compatible with the one you are with. Do not try to look for the perfect man or woman. Perhaps they would be looking for the perfect counterpart also - then what would each of you do? [laughter] I tease you a little!

Trust your heart to follow your own guidance - your own deeper awareness, and you will find a reciprocal element in your life with another to help you wear off the rough edges of the beautiful shining jewel of life that you are.

*Two years ago I experienced a great love for someone and also a great deal of fear. I didn't know how to go further with the love, we separated and I experienced depression and the feeling of dying. Last year I started feeling better, but lately I have been experiencing pain in my chest, my heart, and I've been having the feeling of dying again.*

You have been moving through a lot of psychic awareness and that is the process you are struggling with: how to come to grips with your increased sensitivity, your understanding of love on a deeper level. In a sense, you are doing battle with some of the old psychological fears - elements of your consciousness that deny your own Divinity. Elements that say, "No, it is not possible that I too am Divine. I would rather be in my limited mind." That is the personality self.

It is rather normal, by the way, for the outer mind to function in resistance to its greater sense of self-acceptance. Are you able to express love with a few that you feel rather close to, in a way that is non-threatening? In other words, is the sense of love complete in that you know them as friends - is it enough that you have such relationships with a few?

*Yes.*

When the love comes, and you feel the fear of dying, is it not because you want to grasp that love? That you want to say, "This is mine? I want this other person to be mine?" The process of the ego's death - which you fear and embrace at the same time - is partly what you are moving through. I can reassure you that the ego will not die; it will simply have a better sense of its own beingness in relationship to the greater Self. In that greater Self you do not need to possess anyone. It is enough to learn to know yourself and out of that exists free easiness to be with others.

In closing, please recognize you exist in this dimension of your flesh at one level of your consciousness, but on a very broad level, you are operating simultaneously on many levels of consciousness and you have a great deal of friendship with those who act as teachers or guides for you. Not that they should be worshipped - recognize them as your friends. They are happy to be involved in your living.

Rather than thinking life is bleak and there are many problems, start to think a bit that life is as a friendship, and many levels of friendship wait to be explored. Many levels of love, of trust, of deepening will come to be present for you. Have time to share deeply with those you love, but have time also to meditate and reflect on the Spiritual essence of all things. If sadness comes, welcome it as a gift. If joy comes, welcome that as a gift. Do not feel that you have to put yourself in the polarity of good or bad experience.

Be more the witness of the sense of timelessness that may walk with you as you move through life in this very quick embodiment. What is a span of 6ty or one hundred years? It is very quick. Why not enjoy the process? As you do that, you bless yourself and you bless others. The human race begins to wake up now. It is a time of quickening. The time flow in a subjective sense is accelerating, so much will come up from within that needs to be clarified. You may feel a very intense process moving you at times. When you feel that great intensity, try to get your body into nature where timelessness is more easily perceived than in the intensity of the city.

There are many ways, many tools, many techniques. Let healing be that which you explore. Let love be deep and honest. Do not try to force love - just allow it. Rather than try to *make* yourself perfect - as though there is some stereotype image of who and what you should be - remember the child within. The Christ, the Buddha that lies within you will be more easily blessed into awakening or quickening to the conscious mind by allowing the child to have freedom and flexibility.

I want to say that again: Enlightenment is a wonderful state of consciousness, with much humor, happiness and joy - as the child - with no thought of how serious and important it is to be enlightened! [laughter]

You are eternal beings now and forever. The Divine heritage is always upon you. Lighten up. Let it flow. It has been our joy to share with you.

# Meditation

*Visualize a beautiful child of light within you.*
*Begin to breathe in a deep way,*
*but naturally.*

*Ask the child to come out and play.*
*Bring the child out and do a little bow.*
*Start to dance a bit with the child*
*in your thoughts.*

*Feel the playfulness of the child*
*moving through your feet,*
*touching the earth.*

*A sense of longing comes up,*
*that your hands may express.*
*Touch the earth and feel the wind,*
*the air,*
*the sky,*
*with your hands,*
*with your face.*

*You find yourself*
*at a beautiful seashore with the child.*
*You both lay down on a beach blanket.*
*You lay down and feel the sun.*
*Feel the golden light of the sun*
*flowing in you and through you.*

*You are the daughter of the most high,*
*the son of the most high.*
*And the other sons and daughters,*

*both in the Spirit and in the flesh,*
*will more and more come to be your friends.*

*Be aware of the simple joys of life.*
*Therein lies happiness.*
*Therein lies your true consciousness.*

*God bless you.*

# Chapter 13

# On Quieting The Monkey Mind

*Many people are feeling themselves changing nowadays, and often they have openings - what one might term "psychic" experiences. Some find that these openings, these experiences, are a bit frightening. Please speak about the significance of these experiences and how people can best deal with them.*

Well, we would begin with the question, "What is your mindset?" If you think that God should be as an old man in the heavens - which I am confident you do not - then your experience of God comes in a way that can only be different from your expectations. It is in opposition to your mindset. More to the point, however, everyone wants to be suddenly enlightened. Yesterday would be not soon enough! In your desire for enlightenment, sometimes you force the centers open. It is wonderful to have the opening come, but a little patience lends a lot of beauty.

So in your desire for quickening of your Spiritual consciousness, look first to the body. What are you doing with your body? Are you clothing it with the right food for thought, the right food for the physical body? Are you giving exercise to the physical body? The physical vehicle needs to become a temple. And once you have the experience of your body as a temple, you will not be frightened - you will be overjoyed.

Of course, to find balance you may need to experience imbalance, so that you can recognize balance when it comes. You will go through your levels of resistance - there is no shortcut. But if you can look upon the process with a bit of detachment you will see what might be termed in your vernacular the "monkey mind." That is the term we like to use for the part of the mind that is always critical, loves to worry, is constantly telling you that you are not doing well enough. Begin to make friends with that monkey. Begin to talk to it, to win it over a little to a deeper way of thought. Never think that the monkey will stop being a monkey - it will always be a monkey. But, you can stand aside and say, "Oh, I see that part of my mind getting caught in worry or frustration. I will look a little deeper." Or just share your fear. Speak to another, saying in honesty, "This is what is coming up for me." You may find your fear dispelled very quickly, rather than holding on to it for so long that you keep turning it over and over.

*We have all heard, "I create my own reality." How does it work that somehow I am manufacturing my own experiences, including misery and pain? Explain this choice that we have to grow through pain or grow through joy.*

Well, if you want to listen to the monkey, the monkey will of course insist upon pain. It likes the conflict. That is its primary programming, to create separation. You have individualized yourself through many lives, and that is a wonderful gift. The monkey has served you very well but now it is time to take another look. Now it is time for reintegrating with your deeper Self. How does pain serve you for this? Because out of pain you stop becoming so enamored of the ego. You go a little deeper, where there is no pain, and there you find the greater unity.

But why not do it through joy? That is the question. Joy is there if you allow it. You *do* create your reality on the deepest levels of consciousness. But that does not mean that you understand it on the outer level. On the outer level the mind would say, "Oh, God, why is this happening to me?" The outer mind wants to blame everyone else. The inner mind has no blame, no competition, for

180

self or anyone else. It just exists in the deepest levels of integration.

So, you have a *choice* of where you will align yourself. Do you want to be in harmony with your deeper Self? This may seem hard to the ego mind, but to the deeper Self it results in joy. So ask yourself, "Am I worthy of experiencing joy? Do I allow myself to receive what I want? Or do I, in the moment when it comes, turn aside from the gift that would be there and somehow say I am not worthy. Do I somehow throw a "monkey-wrench," as you say, "into the works and create something different, just to prove I can do it?" Of course you can do it, but why not let the joy come.

*Do you have any suggestions for supporting that process?*

Well, look around you and see what others move through. If you find you are stuck in your drama, in your pain, find someone else who is also stuck. Help them out of their stuck place. While you were focused on them, you changed your attention from your need to theirs. You have moved into a state of service, and have become unstuck in the process. Looking to see the needs of others shows you at the same time what is your own true need. It is so very simple, but not so simple in words because words make for quick analysis. It is a process, an evolution. You need to trust the process to move you as you most deeply desire. Some degree of this is what might be called a state of prayer, a state of meditation, a state of inner questing or questioning. The answers come at the same time.

*Please say a bit about meditation and its use for bringing the different levels of the mind, the emotions and the Spirit together.*

You are Spirit, you have always been Spirit, you will always be Spirit. The deeper mind has this knowledge, this recognition. As you move with more joy, more devotion, more sense of inner seeking into prayer and meditation, what you seek for begins to come. It may not come instantly. It may seem very slow, and you may wonder if anything is going on, but gently within you, you are allowing for deeper integration. As the deeper mind opens, your sensitivity increases and you begin to see more of the games that you play with yourself. You begin to see more of the psychological patterns that you are perpetuating, which serve you not. So you see more of what you feel pained by, but in the same process you are also opening up to more compassion, which extends to yourself and draws others toward you. You can begin to get a sense that, "I am in this process, just as is everyone else." We are all in it together, and there is really no problem that cannot be met by more understanding, more compassion. So, in a real sense, you are opening to the universe to receive you. And as you open to yourself in that way, you also receive the universe.

Look within, and find there the still, small voice. Discover the quietude that is present, even though you may be in the center of a cyclone. In its own way, change is the beauty of Self being revealed. But if your outer personality resists, you may think no beauty is present. You can choose to stop resisting, then look around: you will find beauty everywhere!

Chapter 14

# Addiction - Spiritual Hunger?

*It is our joy to share with you,*
*that each of you might find what you seek.*

*The reality of your hunger for life*
*is found within you,*
*though you may search in many places,*
*many embodiments,*
*to find truth.*

*It abides within*
*and has always done so.*

*The conscious search*
*may seem to be "out there" somewhere,*
*but in reality*
*it is a circle back to your deeper knowing.*

Addiction is simply allowing the self to experience energy in a variety of ways, some which serve you; some which do not. The purpose, then, is to experience life in a pattern that serves. If you look very closely, everything in life might be seen as an addiction. Addiction could be described as desire unfulfilled; desire for love, desire for awakening, desire for consciousness, desire for the Spirit.

The outer mind, the personality self, is very deeply programmed to lead you through many adventures. It has chosen to manifest in the physical kingdom as a personality which allows you to experience individualization; your separation from one another, your separation from time and space. The outer mind has a very wonderful role to fulfill in allowing the ego expression and choice. You allow yourself individualization through different times in the body, through living both as man and woman, through rich and poor, through deep, as well as shallow, states of awareness. You experience all of those states in order to choose what you would hold to and what you would let go.

In an ultimate sense life is a letting go. It is letting go of the addiction. It is letting go of the desires that serve you not. It is letting those things which do serve reside within and harmonize with you. If you look at it in that fashion, it becomes a pattern of growth. It is not good or bad, or good versus evil. That is a favorite trick of the outer mind; to create dichotomy, paradox and separation. It loves to say, "This is good, that is bad." You might more honestly say, "This serves me better than that. I have already done that so I no longer need the lesson. This serves me better."

What, then, are the attributes of addiction which serve you not? What are the blockages you hold onto for fear of letting them go? Look at the body. Look at the mind and the emotions. Look at your Spiritual essence. In each area you will find those things that work

184

in a positive sense and those that do not. Look at the heavily refined foods you put in the body, foods devoid of life force. They have no true essence of Divinity remaining. You have the skeleton of the essence. You have the dead flesh, you might say, of that which you call food, whether it be plant or animal. It is generally not filled with life vitality.

If you eat the dead flesh, you get a certain amount of energy from it. You get the proteins, vitamins and minerals it may contain. But you do not usually receive the enzyme activity - which is the closest analogy to the life essence. So it is quite simple - if you eat a lot of processed foods, you lose energy. So you try to find energy in "pick me up" stimulants such as coffee and teas with caffeine and cigarettes. If you get too "up," you look for something to calm you down, such as alcohol or drugs. The refined sugar in your abundant supply of food is also a drug, and one day you will so proclaim it in your society.

If you want to get comfortable with your body, which is a wonderful thing to do, start to train it to enjoy the foods that carry the life force. It need not be a heavy discipline. If you allow yourself the joy of experiencing how the body may feel, you will not want to go back to your old habits because you will have a much clearer feeling.

If you drink coffee, for example, you get an artificial boost, but it is a muddy energy. The caffeine quickens your body's response, but that which gives it flavor, the burning of the beans, acts as an irritant in the system and creates its own form of stimulus. It creates a muddying of the water of your energy. It creates irritation and fear. It creates a sense of paranoia. So you get a high, then you get a low. The low is lower than before you started. It may take a long time for it to affect your body, or it may affect it quickly. For some, coffee in moderation may be a medicine that does not bother

185

them. But for most, it tends to burn out the pancreas. It overly addresses the detoxification function of the liver and creates disharmony in the body, most particularly in the emotional response. So if you drink a lot of coffee, do not be surprised if you feel easily irritated with others.

Each body is different. Some are more sensitive than others. The mind has a great capacity to affect your feeling state. Some may drink poison, literally, and it will not affect them. But why push the body with these more gentle forms of poison of which we speak? Try to eat the foods that serve you. Get away from the quick fix, and you will have more energy. You will start to feel happy in your body. Then your body will not want the things that induce a quick acceleration of energy. In this more gentle state, you will feel the balance in your emotional self.

If you are very sensitive, one of the ways you may try to decrease your sensitivity is with alcohol. Many people who are open psychically, more than they realize, quickly make alcohol their friend because it reduces sensitivity. It is also a boost to the blood sugar. And the sugar element creates havoc in the body and produces addiction. So rather than eating sugar in the sweets, perhaps you have it in the alcohol - you have a beer or something. It gives the body a sense of well-being, because it gives a little energy of blood sugar. But it creates its own form of addiction, both physically and psychologically.

As you look at anything that may be a physically addictive substance, try to see beyond it and understand the desire behind it. The desire is to experience more vital energy, that in its balanced state, may be translated as love. The desire is love. It is to feel loving of your body, your heart, your mind, and your emotions. It is to feeling loving toward others and loving of your Spiritual awakening. That is the true desire under your outer action. It is a wonderful desire, well worth fulfilling.

Be the witness to your process. Be the observer and analyze it in a way that is not harsh and critical. See how the body responds, what ups and downs it goes through psychologically and physically. Observe the times of the day you feel low on energy and try taking an afternoon nap, rather than a quick fix of coffee or sugar.

These are all ways to work with feeling better. Perhaps the most intensifying process you can utilize is daily meditation and prayer, your own point of engaging with the Spirit. As you begin to feel the well-being that slowly accumulates, the sense of centering and balance, and deeper love which comes, your body will speak clearly to you. It will tell you what works and what does not. You may need to work and move through many old programs - sometimes strong childhood programs.

Whatever way you choose to center, know that you touch more deeply then, the "hem of the garment", the place of healing within. Your own strength and courage will manifest in such a way that you feel good about yourself, so you can stop the critical mind and its chatter. You can stop analyzing, contrasting, throwing everything into categories and always making yourself wrong. It is a complex and yet quite simple experience of life.

If you have long been in an environment in which others have some form of addictive pattern in their personality, in their behavior, you may discover that you are the "fixer." You want to rush in as the savior and try to help them. You want to try to make them well, even though you may recognize that others may need to complete the cycle they are going through in order to work it out, burn it out, and try it to the final point.

What happens when one "hits bottom" psychologically and

physically in the sense of societal standards? What happens when you hit the very bottom? You find God. The ego finally gives up and says, "Okay, I need help." That is a wonderful place to come to. I do not suggest you do it on purpose, but if you do reach that point, say in yourself, "Okay God, there is something larger than me I need to connect with, I need to be a part of, in order to get myself out of this hole." And you find God. Somehow, someway, He comes. Sometimes in your society it has been called grace; the feeling of essence, the feeling of forgiveness of self and others.

The rock bottom reality is that you are perfect. You are Divine and some sense of that begins to filter into the mind and emotions. The personality stops judging itself so harshly and gives you more freedom. Then you can get on about your business of awakening.

Center yourself within. Find the tools that work. Find the time of counsel with others. Begin to see beneath the surface. Do not let the facade of the ego - your own or anyone else's - blind you to the fact that everyone is essentially the same, everyone is at a point of unity. And it is that point where true salvation, awakening and Spiritual consciousness takes place. It is in that point of union that you feel yourself to be most whole.

Let your own Divinity emerge. Do not be frightened to allow it. Perhaps the greatest fear of the ego is to experience Divine presence, because the ego is convinced it will dissolve in that contact. But it will not dissolve. It will be gently transformed. The ego is an aspect of your individualization, like the tip of the iceberg. It is a great gift the universe gives you through the process of physical embodiment. So you will not lose your identity, your individuality, your uniqueness. You will gain the universe in the process.

You are all immediately, equally Divine, and you have never been

188

any other way. It is beyond the personality mind, the ego mind, to deal with that. But think about it anyway. Get a sense of it in your meditation times.

I think that is enough. We will now look at questions that may have been precipitated in your thoughts by what we have suggested.

*I have a question about the general addictiveness of society, and the increasing awareness of the ways we look outside ourselves for happiness and well-being. As a result, more people are engaging in forms of recovery such as 12-step programs or self-support programs outside of formal channels. What is going on with this, and where is it going in the future?*

What is essentially taking place is that people are waking up. And in the waking up, they start to shed those things which bind them. As they awaken, those things fall away. The patterns which allow that to take place are exemplified well in the 12-step programs. These programs speak of integration of the personality, of greater self-respect and respect for others. They speak of touching the Divinity and sharing with others in the process.

In these programs, addictive patterns which create separation and a sense of not loving self, are met with love and understanding. The love, then, is the author of awakening. That is truly what takes place more and more. It is a time of awakening. You stand on the threshold of a new age in consciousness in which addiction, as you know it, shall not exist.

The reason much of this is happening outside of formalized training programs is that whenever energy gets caught in an organizational structure, it gets a bit crystallized. Organizations are necessary. They help to bring focus to things that need to be accomplished, but many times the guiding light, the inspiration of the one who began the process, may become lost. The personality loves to put things into categories, into boxes. It loves to organize, to somehow improve things, when in truth, it is a movement of the Spirit. The Spirit is not bound by the boxes of society, or the organizational structures. It flows up. It is from the grass upward - grass roots, as you would say.

More and more, people will feel themselves empowered as they awaken out of their sleep state. That is what you are feeling - that graduation, that shift. And that which you invoke in yourself and others is very positive in the movement of loving self. That is all there really is. Is there not anything that does not come back to loving self?

*It seems that the 12-step approach is one of the only viable ways to address the issue of addiction, and it appears that the "old way," such as taking your sick, addicted body to a therapist or a counselor to be healed, is completely outmoded. Is this true?*

What you are sensing is simply the ego stepping aside. In the past, if you took your body to one who was the "healer", the process functioned primarily at a psychological level. The therapist said, "This is where you are," put a title on it, and that supposedly described your process. The issue was intellectually and psychologically examined and dealt with, but it was not usually addressed with the Spirit. Those who are successful have been so because they are awakened to the Spiritual essence. They have brought empathy forward, a total surrounding of the person in the sense that they are not an "addict," they are not a thing, a category, but a being of infinite possibilities. And those who have been extremely successful, such as Carl Jung and others, have been the explorers of their own day in terms of human consciousness. As the patterns they discovered were explored by others, sometimes

190

those who used them awoke to their own potential, and other times the ideas became crystallized as a form, a pattern, which was accepted.

The real point is the issue of whether or not the ego can capture and control the process, categorize it and place it into a box, or whether it is a continual new blossoming, a new springtime with each flower and bud opening to its own beauty, no two being quite the same. That is what works. And whether you call it "12-step," or "3-step," or use religious terminology, what it amounts to is allowing compassion to have room to function.

Compassion is the great equalizer. It takes away the pain, the suffering, the doubt, the fear, the loss. Where perfect love exists, fear does not exist. Fear is the illusion, the shadow. Love is the reality. And individuals are beginning to empower themselves to recognize the right to experience and share compassion or love. And when you come together with common purpose, you empower one another. You see the issues that have brought you down, and you empower each other to move past them, to stop judging, to stop getting caught in categories saying, "I am a this, I am a that." That is what is happening, and it is quite profound. It is a move of the Spirit. More and more, the awakening consciousness of humanity is beginning to gain momentum. It is power, beyond any other power.

*I see some children who have developed addictive patterns as a defense against not feeling loved. Is the addiction a defense, in relation to their own Spiritual awakening?*

Well, children are quite sensitive, and are usually very open on a psychic level. If there is abundant love in the surroundings of its upbringing, then the child matures in a beautiful natural way. If there is a lack of love, then, as you have read in your Scriptures, the sins of the parents shall be visited upon the children. If you look at sin as not knowing, as a lack of understanding, that is precisely what takes place. The child is so sensitive from the time of gestation, all that develops in the womb to the birth affects that child, who is very open and receptive to the energy that is there.

The biggest help for any child is to be with those who love themselves. The child who grows up in an atmosphere where there is little love may feel that the only way to experience energy - which is a basic hunger - is to do something "naughty," to get attention in a negative way, to create patterns of personality that may not be pleasant for others, but at least gets some kind of recognition. Any energy is better than none. That is where the psychological defense mechanisms enter. That is how the baseline of the personality operates.

If there is a lot of mental and emotional imbalance in the surroundings, many things can take place. First of all, know that the child is a fully mature soul with its own internal process of clearly recognizing what exists, what is balanced, what is not. Some children become tremendously strong in their defense against the negative energy, the anger, the fear and doubts of others. For some, it becomes too subtle and too integrated into their personality to separate. There are defense mechanisms you may not know how to remove, but the power of the mental, emotional, physical process of healing can go deep and find the keys that gently turn and allow the child to access their own deeper knowledge.

That is something in which you can participate. Go into a meditative state. Ask that there might be a flow of healing of loving energy through you, augmented by your teachers, that is balanced and brought forward to the higher Self of the one for whom you pray. Ask that that individual's higher Self use the energy in whatever way is appropriate. That is a deep level of communion. You will share telepathically, higher Self to higher Self, though your personality may not be aware of that.

Allow your efforts to be well past the point where you create expectations and then feel frustrated because you were not able to do what you thought you should. Know that the universe works, and that is what you are allowing to take place. You are tapping into something larger than yourself in the personality sense, and assisting another to do the same. It empowers you to see more of the unlimited potential available, so your own healing goes forward in the process.

*If an individual - whether a child or an adult - could more clearly see negative situations and express their anger appropriately, would they be less likely to be addictive?*

That depends on the situation. Healing may come through an expression of anger. It is much more direct sometimes to express it and let it flow, let it get over with, than it is to keep stuffing it. But it depends on the situation. Sometimes the expression of anger is like lighting a fuse to a keg of dynamite. Some adults may be imbalanced enough that the anger expressed may simply trigger more of their own emotional response, and the situation goes from bad to worse.

It would depend on the environment. If the soul sees clearly and deeply what is present, and that clarity moves to the conscious mind, then they have moved past the need of angry expression. But this is a very difficult thing to express in your language, because what generally happens is that one then thinks, "Oh, I should have enough insight, I should be Spiritual enough, I should recognize what's going on clearly enough that I don't feel any anger," when in truth, they do feel anger. I do not wish to suggest that you

193

should deny those feelings. I would like to suggest that if there is total clarity, anger does not exist.

If it is necessary for the anger to come forward, a psychological process may help bring that out. But anger can be a tremendous hook. You can go through your whole life angry at someone, and, whether you express it or not, still feel angry. Expressing it may bring it up so you may work with it a little more, but to just feel anger is to still be hooked. It is a step along the way - it is not a final step.

*Both of my parents were alcoholics. I believe that we choose our family and I wonder - why would a child choose to be born to alcoholic parents?*

The possibilities might be many. Ultimately, the realization of "why" would have to come from the Soul knowledge of the individual. But you may, in your own expanded consciousness, be able to see why others have chosen various situations, and that may give you a hint as to why you chose it.

Ultimately it is to allow Divinity to fully flower. Divinity often picks very tight, restricted situations to embody through in order to feel the resistance that the light may more brightly shine. For example, if you observe someone such as Helen Keller you might ask, "Why would she pick a body born in such limitation?" She was a very old soul. She came in the body for her own purpose - to feel the limitation of the physical senses, and to move past that limitation to find the Divinity flowing through her. She also brought hope to many, helping others to recognize that, in spite of any limitations the physical body may have, still there is a total being behind the body. So she helped to bring more compassion and she experienced an awakening to compassion for herself.

You might use that analogy in your own situation, or that of others. For you find more and more that compassion touches you, as that, above all things, for which you hunger. Is that not true?

*Yes, that is very true.*

So you have answered your own question, is that not so? You have the answers. When you find a question within you, therein always lies the answer.

*When you look at the world today compared with one hundred years ago, is there more addiction now, or is it simply recognized more as a problem now?*

Well, there is more consciousness now, therefore there is more energy and more ability to use energy. There is the desire to use energy, and in that desire, the addictions may seem more prevalent because everybody is feeling the movement of time quickened. The personality of every person is feeling their process speeded up. So there may be substance abuse, there may be psychological patterns that are addictive, but there is a tremendous under-girding hunger for the Spirit. That is what the addiction rolls on. There is more energy being made available within the heart, soul and mind of each individual. And the ways to quicken that may be found artificially, or they may be found in a deep response to self. As they are found artificially, then you have more addiction. Technology helps. It makes many things available, so you can get addicted on all kinds of things.

*So there is more addiction now because there is more Spiritual hunger?*

Let us just say there is more energy, so you are more aware of where the imbalances lie, as well as where the positive aspects are.

Three or four hundred years ago, most people were not thinking about some of these finer points. They were just making it through life as best they could. There is progression. It may not seem as such, but there is progression. And as you progress, you may need opportunities to deal with energy in ways that are not always balanced. There is always a step-by-step process. Each one has to find the perimeters of how they will deal with energy and how they will begin to experience their own Divinity.

*I have been working on quitting smoking. I have many tools I know I should use, such as tapes and books, yet I don't utilize them.*

Do you allow yourself to enjoy the power of oxygen? That would be your solution; more oxygen in the lungs, more activity that is physical to allow the body to draw in the oxygen. The more you do that, the more you will feel the quickening of your own energy, and the less you will feel the need of the nicotine to give you that energy fix.

By the way, smoking helps to ground you. Did you know that? The smoking is a bit of a grounding part of your experience. So you cannot just take it away. You need to go ahead and get the real thing, and then you can drop it. You can do all kinds of things; walking, running, playing, dancing, swimming. All of those things involve the heart and lungs, and allow the body to feel physically more active. You will feel the empowerment of yourself in a beautiful way, and the slow dropping of the smoking can then take place. Just be in nature. Be physically active. Do things that are physical and vital which make you happy. That is the best approach. Take a little outing. Go on a camping trip. Go sleep outside once a week somewhere. Do not always sleep with a roof over your head. Let nature start to sing for you. Then you will feel grounded, and the planet becomes a living entity - Divine in its energy source.

We should now close. Perhaps you would like to join in a moment of meditation.

# Meditation

*Center yourself.*

*Allow a sense of Spiritual presence*
*in your thought,*
*in the recognition*
*that many have gathered whom you see not.*

*They bring their energy*
*and join with you in this meditation.*

*Begin to feel light flowing through your body,*
*up from the planet.*

*Now sense a radiant energy of light*
*coming down from the heavens,*
*flowing through you,*
*meeting,*
*sharing.*

*Feel the awakening*
*in each cell of the body.*

*Gently,*
*in your mind's eye,*
*see yourself as illumined,*
*filled with light.*

*Within the center of the room,*
*begin to sense a more intensified field of energy.*
*Heaven and earth sharing light,*
*forming a radiant column of energy.*

*In yourself,*
*find something of awkwardness,*
*some point of not letting go,*
*some personality trait,*
*some relationship with self or others,*
*whatever it is that you feel is not healed*
*and which feels burdensome.*

*Mentally place that burden*
*in the column of light.*

*Let it become an image that you bring there.*
*Let the light fill it and begin to transform it.*
*Ask that love and healing flow through you.*

*Out of the center of the room*
*walks a teacher bearing a wrapped gift.*
*Receive the gift.*
*Gently open it.*
*Let the gift become your own.*

*Begin to sense that earth and heaven*
*together form your home,*
*that you simultaneously exist in all dimensions.*

*Know that you walk in the light of the Spirit,*
*and as you desire self-knowledge to come,*
*it will come.*

*It has been our great joy to share with you.*

*God bless you.*

Chapter 15

# The Future Of Education

*God bless you.*
*It is our joy that we might share with you.*

*You seek,*
*in your own way,*
*to overcome the habit patterns of the past.*
*And the limitations of thought*
*that others hold,*
*as to the advancement of society.*
*And how there might be a deeper integration*
*within each one*
*who comes into your sphere of influence.*

*You desire a broadening of outreach*
*beyond your immediate contact,*
*to those who are young in years*
*but old in the body of wisdom*
*that you might call the Spirit.*
*They have young bodies and old souls,*
*so to speak.*

*Allow a sense of your own gladness in life*
*to permeate what you do,*
*in spite of the difficulties of this time*
*through which mankind moves*
*as a transition into a deeper awakening.*

*Have the gladness*
*of your own creative capacity*
*working with you.*

*The happiness and the joy,*
*which take you beyond*
*the troubles and problems of the moment,*
*into a deeper sphere*
*of influence within yourself.*

*We have many questions today, mainly focused around the future of education. I think we might start off by asking this: We know that many children in school today - many children - are not at all achieving their own potential...*

They are bored.

*They're bored, yes. Would you please tell us the basic reasons for this, and of course, what might be done to change the situation?*

Well, the reasons are many but the basic reason is that there is a deep awareness of the Soul being brought forth now, and unless that is spoken to, unless that is alluded to directly, the real sense of joy and excitement to be in the body is not tapped and therefore boredom sets in. That is the real reason. It is not just the schooling; it is the parental attitudes, it is the influence of your newspapers, your televisions particularly; all of that. The real reason for the boredom is that society, as a whole, has not yet awakened to the point that the Spirit within is being addressed directly. Education will be the key to that process taking place, and in many ways there may be children who come forth with the power of insight naturally present, not having unlearned it. In many cases what you are trying to do then, is teach what is already present, and to awaken that true excitement of living and learning and growing.

The future of education will move in the direction of integrating the deeper aspects of the mind. The intellect and the attitudes that are associated now with technological achievement - the ability to recall facts and place them in order and achieve a sense of logical process whereby reasoning takes place - that will be finely tuned and continue to be developed. It is a balancing of one aspect of the mind. It is good in that it does reach out to search the available perimeters of knowledge and wisdom in the physical plane, but it is not enough in it itself. The attributes that you would term artistic

203

endeavor; that which is creative in art and music, that which is creative in philosophical pursuit - not just the philosophy of the moment; to take either side and see how well you can spread the wings of your intellect and reason, but rather to touch within the place of what you feel this to mean. When all of that is brought more into direct harmony, you then will be teaching the insight that the whole being may address.

The body will be seen as a particularly useful way of energizing consciousness. The importance of the wholeness of food, environment and exercise will be recognized - that just because one has a young body does not mean it is being programmed well in the physical sense of food and environment. That shows up quickly in the later years, but in the young years the food and such may not be obvious as to the effect that it has. But the sharpness of perception, the clarity of instinct, all of that becomes important. And I know that your schools cannot control the home environment, but it will become a factor in time. The whole process of education will go back into the home.

*Could you give examples of a couple things that might be specific things that might be done in the classroom, let us say in the early grades, that would be toward this end that you are speaking about?*

Teaching of basic meditations. Working with visualizations. Encouraging the romance of the intuition and the intellect combined. Teaching little games that might point out the ability of the mind to transcend the limitations with which it is normally associated. There are many techniques - very simple techniques - that will quickly disprove the idea that minds do not interface. So you begin to teach that there is that instinctive sense of communication just below the surface. Not that everyone has to run around trying to read everyone's mind, but the emotional tone, the content of the environment becomes quickly real when that is acknowledged. So again, the accessibility of instinctual knowledge is deepened. And at a young age it is already present to a high degree. Unfortunately, many aspects of education, as well as the peer group and the surrounding family group of the child, will kill any natural talent in the intuitive sense. That can be turned around.

The teaching in schools can be a very real tool to allow that. This is not something that takes hours and hours of each day. It might be something that is one program a day, one hour period a day. That is not difficult to do. Certainly some sense of integrating the body into the process, such as basic yoga postures where the development of muscle is not just towards sports for example, towards achieving a quick victory over one's opponent, but that there is a sense of bringing the mind into the cells, bringing the awareness into the body. And body awareness will teach diet, for example. If body awareness is deepened, then for example, sugar and the candy bars and such will be understood to do what they do by the individual, rather than laying on as a rule or a regulation: "You do this and you don't do that." You teach the individual to trust themselves, to trust their point of perception. That is a tremendous gift to give. Much more important than absorbing facts is absorbing the ability to trust one's own basic knowing. That is all available to the very young, provided their parents do not turn around and take it all away again.

*When you say "very young," how young are you meaning?*

I think from age two or three and up. It would be modified at the very young age, but when you have children at five or six or seven years of age, their natural instinctive awareness is present. It is strong. And if they are allowed to continue in that awareness, then they continue in their natural awakening, rather than having to relearn it later, after it has been shut down, as so often is the case.

205

*Do you have ideas about how that can be incorporated in a very young school program that is offered, like in our kindergarten programs?*

Take five to fifteen minutes to do some guided imagery, to take children to a special place of their own finding where they might feel good about themselves. If the body has a little ache or pain, they might be able to find a way to tap energy to resolve the ache or pain. Basic techniques of self-knowing are rather simple in their essence. Truth is simple.

*So do you think that these can be incorporated in our present day programs that we are offering?*

Yes. Quietly. It would not step on too many toes if those who are teaching have themselves, relatively speaking at least, integrated their own knowingness so that it flows through them not as something they read - not that there is anything wrong with reading, it gives you ideas and concepts - but it is not something you dryly repeat. It is something you bring into your own language and your feeling. In guided imagery, for example, the quality of knowing that opens in the student will respond to the quality of knowing in the teacher, directly. Therefore, if the teachers has within themselves integrated the feeling of energy of meditation, of insight, that energy communicates. It is not verbal, but it is entirely tangible to the mind of the student. Not every student of course. But basically, the quality of energy we are speaking of is easily demonstrated through one who has tapped that quality in themselves. It is not there just as an intellectual concept.

*At the kindergarten level, parents are often wanting more linear kind of information, more factual information, more and more so all the time. How much can a young mind absorb? How much*

206

*should we be teaching of that linear type of information at a young age?*

The linear information will be absorbed and integrated more deeply and will actually be more accessible and useful with a mind that is being trained in the aspects of which we speak. That is not a direct answer to your question. I just want you to know that this does not add more to an already bursting situation so that they are on overload. Quite the reverse; if there was more of the integration that we speak of first, then the mind would be more able to absorb the linear models as well, as long as they are interesting. If they are boring, then the mind will say, "That is boring," because it will perceive directly that that is so. What you are teaching then, is the ability to shift perspective; to access different levels of consciousness; and to start to sift and program what is important to the individual. Not to become just a vast reservoir, in which everything is poured, as on magnetic tape, but rather to begin to start shifting insights and pursue the things that are particularly interesting to the child. I think that is one of the attributes of education that will open up. Each one has tremendous capability of learning, at what you might consider an accelerated rate, as long as it holds their interest.

Not all children would be learning the same thing at the same time. There would be a basic overview of information and then the ability to learn directly on their own. And this is the point where some of your computer technology will begin to interface through programmed learning, depending on the program. I want to emphasize that the computer is only as good as the program itself. If it is very insightful and interesting and would hold the interest of the child; then it becomes their own individual tutor, so to speak. That becomes more technologically oriented. That is an aspect, a tool, a useful tool, but in itself it is not just the only form or focus.

*I have had the suspicion that the way we teach the linear subjects - mathematics, reading, and so on - would be different if the child had, let us say, a prior exposure to intuition development.*

It would be quite different, that is true. There is nothing wrong with some of the techniques that are used today, in that you may have one teacher and a relatively small group - perhaps eighteen would be a peak - so that the interfacing between the students and the teacher still has some individual context. Fourteen might be better. The smaller the group the more intense the individual focus. If the intuitive instincts were present, the ability to combine the knowledge of the teacher, with the kind of programming that might be possible through computers, would add variability and interest to the program. The intuitive Self would grasp what it needs and be able to link many different aspects. Computer technology is such that in very short order the amount of data available will be tremendous and quickly accessible. The teaching format will also become less linear simply because of this technology.

The intuitive self will begin to see models of how the mind works, regardless of subject material. The children will begin to see that there are levels of consciousness. When many levels of consciousness are opened simultaneously, the kinds of knowledge that may be brought about are best taught by giving an overview first. For example, in mathematics, you might teach the qualities of insight necessary to understand that there are many possible forms of mathematical structure. The philosophy of mathematics would be taught first and the technology second, so that the child would know that in the practical universe you could deal with Euclidean geometry, but in the universe where there is travel to the stars and such, you deal with a geometry where there are no straight lines; there are only curved lines. In this way you begin to open the door to the tremendous variety of information that is available in your advanced degree status - college and beyond.

That overview in the simpler form could easily be made available to the students, and many of those students would then be able to access knowledge already present in them from past life endeavors. And if you want to get really refined, you would begin to have a mapping of the past life experience of each individual child, and ascertain on a psychic level their particular points of strength and interest. This calls for intuitive people to be working directly with the children in setting up curriculums which would vary with the children. We are speaking now of an educational program that would really work. It would work so well that what now takes eight to 6teen years to teach will take two to three years. I know that sounds impossible, but it is not.

*How many years will it take for our present society to reach that point?*

We are speaking of sixty years, perhaps, but not more. I see the realm of potentials opening on an individual basis of schooling, perhaps not the universal schooling of the public mind, but on an individual basis, within the next ten to fifteen years. In the next twenty-five years, many would begin to apply these educational processes in the schooling programs, and in a generation it would be the norm. [Trance from April 1989]

*In the present schooling, what subjects are of value to continue teaching and which ones are of no need? Which ones can we eliminate?*

I do not think it is a question of no need, it is simply a question of where the interest lies in the students - that they be given the opportunity to study the basics in terms of verbal skills, technical skills and writing skills. The ability to learn language rapidly is available at a young age. There may even be the introduction of two or three languages taught instinctually, intuitively, in a way that is useful. Just as language is learned in the very young years of waking up the consciousness of the child, of the baby, so also is there the accessibility of two or three languages. Not that there has to be total refinement, but that the mind gets more flexible, given that opportunity. So even the distillation of language down to five or four or 6 years of age begins to be a reality. You have a marvelous opportunity in this culture, to teach Spanish. It would be a second language in your country if it were used. Why not make it available?

These new forms of teaching will require letting go of the concept that "less is more", that the child will be stultified by too much knowledge - as long as there is the allowing of individual interest. One child may dive deeply into mathematics, another into music, another into art.

Tutors, educational programs, computers, teachers, and teacher assistants will all be quite useful. Counselors - both psychic and psychological - would be part of this educational process. Also, it will need to be recognized that there are those in the Spiritual dimension who are the real teachers helping the child awaken, so they would also direct the child's consciousness in a way to allow them the full blossoming of their own potential. So they might blossom early into music, if that is the soul desire. They might blossom into mathematics or the mysteries of science, so to speak. But the language of the soul would begin to direct the individual to seek out other realms of knowledge. Knowledge is energy. Energy and it all connects is a broad spectrum. There is nothing about learning in one area that denies learning in another. As that begins to be accessible, the mind of the child opens quite rapidly.

I do not want to stretch the educational form of the moment too quickly, but I do wish to express the thought that the potential of learning is - I would not want to say instantaneous, but nearly so –

because the language of the past lies close to the consciousness of the individual if allowed. There is tremendous learning that each soul carries prior to embodiment. So what you are really doing is reminding them of what is known, re-awakening what is already there.

*Will the same approaches work with high school to secondary school, or if we also started some work with current secondary kids? Would there be some additional things we would need to do to awaken them in the ways you are talking about?*

All we have suggested could be applied at any age level from advanced college down to the very early years. The real insights are basic and true everywhere, and a small child may be more capable of grasping that than one heavily steeped in the intellectual approach. Unfortunately, the intellect can get in the way because it programs the outer mind that we like to call at times the "monkey" into thinking it has knowledge when it does not have wisdom. It has a learned state of knowledge; it does not yet have integration.

What you are trying to achieve with true education is to allow an integration of the personality with deeper knowledge. And the way to go about that might, in actuality, seem easier beginning with the young mind and bringing that young mind forward. In the sense of how that will work in your culture though, it will probably be introduced in reverse order. College level brought back down to the secondary level, brought back down to the primary levels, the kindergarten, because that is where people see the value of it. But the teachers involved in this process may bring it in anywhere if they are able to instill in themselves that knowledge. When they bring it into their own being, and if they are allowed a certain amount of flexibility, they will begin to bring it into their teaching.

*Can we talk about those teachers? Our present day teachers are*

211

*not equipped, as I see it, to do this with a child. How can we bring teachers who are going to work with these children to that point of knowing what to do with the children?*

The easiest solution would be to begin teaching basic meditation to the teachers. Basic skills of communication at the levels we have been speaking about where there is a certain amount of intuitive training going on. This would not be difficult. It would not be time consuming. The lofty principles of education are to expand the mind. You would simply be following that lofty principle with an additional form. Interestingly enough the basics are simple. The basics *are* simple. And those that are truly drawn to teach are already instinctively psychic. Those drawn to the teaching profession, for the most part, want to make it creative and exciting, and that would use all the technologies available. That would mean the computer terminology would be accessible, the forms would be improved and improved and improved. Video-tapes and such would draw on the best available, and there are tremendous resources available. That would mean that in each schoolroom you would have a media center with a large screen, with high definition televisions so that there is no difficulty reading the information if it is printed. The format would be such that it would be like going to a very fine movie to learn certain areas of specialized knowledge.

*Do you know resources such as this that are available now?*

Look at your public television. There is a lot there. There will be more. It is quickly mushrooming. The media seems to be going to the dogs, is that not so?

*It appears so.*

In truth, the technology will become so widespread that people find that they are saturated with incompetence and will begin to

212

demand competence. So those things which serve the needs of the awakening mind at whatever age, will become available. For example, if you capture on tape, on video-tape, something that has high energy. When that is shown to the individuals present, the surrounding energy that is unseen - the teachers that are present in the Spirit - the consciousness awakening in the child accesses that information that is available, even though it is just something there represented by electrons. The mind at its deeper level is not limited to time and space. I will draw an analogy. Who is the one teaching about the power of myth of which everyone speaks?

*Joseph Campbell.*

That was a video, was it not? If you play that video, and the language is not over the head of the child, the deeper soul responds. It knows that information and can be triggered to a quickening of information already latent, already present.

Each field of knowledge will have spokespersons who have integrated that knowledge so deeply that they draw on the Soul consciousness in such a way that it penetrates the minds of others. That can be made available, and the interesting thing will be that the teacher dealing with all of this, will get inspired by the power of their position to bring truth to the children. It will become exciting for them because they will be accessing their own guidance. They will be finding the creative tools to implement the broader spectrum of energy available. I think what it really speaks of is a true sense of evolution in terms of what is seen now as significant in your society.

I do not think it will take longer than ten years, perhaps eight, but I think not longer than ten years before education itself is seen as the most important thing to which your society can attend. And I know sitting on the sidelines now, as you see the vast image of people moving their consciousness toward money and new houses and new cars and lots of new weaponry, and all that seems wrong with the world, it seems impossible to believe that it can take place.

But you will find that it becomes the truth. That finally, the real resources of the planet are seen as the minds present, rather than those things that you speak of as coal, and oil and steel, and the latest technologies on the computer chips. The minds of individuals are the real resources. Every society will begin to see that the true wealth of the nation and of the world is born in the insight that may be developed, and education becomes the tool, not only for those young in their bodies, but it becomes then the norm to go back to school every two or three years for a semester or so. That would be pretty remarkable, would it not?

The youthfulness of the mind will be seen as something that can always grow - that you need not say that the mind is old because the body has years upon it. You become then a child in the true and beautiful sense of opening to greater wisdom throughout your life.

*In the light of what you are saying, right now a lot of schools are feeling a great deal of pressure to deal with more of the social issues; like the increased divorce rate, the drug problem, and so on. In the light of what you have been saying, do you think that we in schools should be providing some aspects of dealing with those kinds of problems with the children?*

I think that in many ways you can bring a balance of insight, particularly in those things which touch the fabric of your society, and the experiences of the children. That insight is of extreme value. Dealing with day-to-day living is more important than an intellectual understanding of something just at a theoretical level. It has to be brought into practicality. What you are asking, I think though, is not whether it has value, but whether or not the schools

214

have the capacity to do that. It does strain the capacity, but as educators, it would be well to address every level of the developing insight of the personality as much as you can.

Of course some of these social problems hit students very individually, rather than as a group or as a social phenomenon, such as when the child's parents are divorced or something similar.

That might be a time for individual training in the computer technologies and such, that they could pursue quickly their own interest in the field, to develop insight into what is going on. That would be one possibility. Another might be the careful screening of students on a month-to-month basis about what is going on in the home, and the flexibility of at least one class available for everyone to pursue their individual growth process. Some of these students might go into a program where counseling would be available for them. It will be important for them to understand how the mind works, so that if the parents are having difficulty, the children will not take upon themselves a tremendous weight of guilt.

So the quality of what has been popularly termed "creative thinking" or "positive thinking," would be brought forth as an educational format that might be more of a common course for everyone, and then allowing these specialized areas, these windows, on more intensified studies as was necessary, or as interest peaked. The overall form of education would be best served if it had that kind of range and flexibility. It would be particularly useful in those areas you have termed as "ghettos," where the child has the same brilliance of mind as any child anywhere, but the environment in its intensity begins to kill the desire to learn. That might be particularly useful there.

*Did I understand you to suggest that we might have computer*

215

*programs that would be helpful to children that are having these social, emotional problems at an early stage?*

In the development of computer programs, if you take a skilled team of perhaps two or three individuals who have deep insight into the psychology of the developing child and how that mind is impacted by things such as divorce, drugs, or other difficult situations, they would create programs which address these areas quite specifically. That would be invaluable to every child, but it would especially provide those who might be running into difficulties a sense of someone to talk to. I do not want to suggest that a computer replaces individuals - it never will - but the creative capacity, as in a well-written book, is there. And if you put together several well-written books that are keying in, then the child may follow this pattern, because it has that need, another child would follow this pattern, as though simply reading another book. But there would be commonality to the point that there would be referencing back and forth.

I know that is pictorially not difficult to see. It would be like the roots running out of the various branches, with various points of wisdom as apples on the tree, each with their own distinctive quality.

*It has been mentioned that many times we need to bring the color spectrum into teaching and open this up to small children, or children period. Do you have comments on that, how we could bring that into the classrooms as they exist today?*

That would be one of the areas very difficult to teach in a non-intellectual manner if there was not room for insight into the intuition. But if there was a little room for insight into intuition, it would be eminently easy to teach. You could ask someone, "What is the color of anger," for example, and get a consensus. "What is

216

the color of happiness? What does the feeling of the trees in the fall evoke?" What I am suggesting is that there is an instinctual knowledge of colors in relationship to the energies of feelings and emotions and more directly, the insight of the soul seeing auras. All of that could be brought forth in a simple way. I think the child mind would grasp it more easily than those who are in their intellectual wisdom far beyond the child mind. It could become something of a game. The teacher might walk in and say, "What color am I today?" and see what the response is.

Also, working with color in a physical way would allow this knowledge to be brought forth quickly to the children - the use of colors, the blending, the mixing, the sensing of the tremendous vitality in the range of energy that colors represent. Have a practical demonstration. You might have a drawing of the day; someone might pose for a life drawing class, drawing the aura. Let each one draw. See what they see. Things like that. I know that it would be at the infancy stage of development now of most people, just something done for the pure enjoyment - the fun of it.

Perhaps Kirlian photography would be a demonstration of how energy flows around objects, around shafts of light perceived through the fingertips and such as that. It could all be done. And then you could ask the children to "imagine." That would be a good word to use. "If you were imagining, just suppose, here is the hand." The person moves into a state of meditation. "What color radiates around the hand? Just suppose." That kind of an approach.

*Many parents are not ready to use these terms, or hear these terms. How do we go about the education of the parents in the process?*

Very carefully! [laughter] I tease you a little. As long as it can be done in a creative environment where the children are enjoying

217

themselves, it would be simply that in the initial stages you would approach the parents. Those parents who are more open would quickly see what was happening. You might also find those who are violently opposed, and they would have the right to have their children shifted into another classroom if that was necessary.

But I think it is important that you do not water down a program to meet the lowest common denominator. That you retain a sense of, "Here is integrity to developing creative modes of thought." That might be the key word in all the processes we are speaking of. The creativity itself becomes more and more of the valued sense of insight into all forms of education and training. And that creative impulse, then, will flow whether it be a business career the person follows, whether they become a skilled communicator, or whether they become a research scientist. It does not matter. The flowering of creative energy itself is what is significant. The forms in which it is applied become personal choice. And I think that might be the key to the whole format we have been suggesting. Creativity itself becoming invaluable in the awareness that that is where solutions truly come from. So it is a new model of the mind; a new model of processes whereby learning takes place.

You can structure it in theoretical terms or you can bring it into the very quickly grasped experience of most children. And I am speaking now of range of ages - from three to hundred and three - since everyone in their essence, in the best sense, remains a child.

*This issue of freedom of choice in a child seems a little bit tricky. It sounds like you are saying the child should be given total freedom of choice, and I am sure you don't mean that. Is there a way we can draw the boundary line here?*

The percentages involved have to be discerned and determined based on the individual schooling situation. But it could range anywhere from one-third of basic form of learning, basic core of learning knowledge, and two-thirds of freely flowing with individual curriculum, as though the child were following their own individual study program such as you might have in an academic setting of advanced learning. It would be brought down to the level of the child. It could be two-thirds core and one-third of the individual program of study. But I think somewhere in that range you would find an optimum value for the many.

You might occasionally run into one that would be a prodigy. They might take eighty percent of individual learning and the core would be picked up easily in the twenty percent time remaining. And these studies might be of such interest that the child would freely take some home and pursue it there - not because they had to, but because they wanted to.

There would be individual choice rendered by the parents of their particular prerogatives. Sometimes those prerogatives would be of great value and insight, sometimes they might be more of a prejudiced point of reference, but then you would have perhaps a broader spectrum of different types of schools available whereby the child is presented to the various schools. Much as you have now private schooling, only it would be more public schooling set in various stages of development. Actually, not so much stages of development as in 1, 2, 3, 4 - basic to advanced - but stages of development as into particular interests and areas of focus. That brings the spectrum of even more diversity, which at the moment perhaps you do not want to address. But all of that could be dealt with later.

I think a particular insight might be the choices derived, particularly through psychic means. That there would be those skilled and trained to be advocates of the right forms of education for the child - that might carry a weight of significance. You will hit a point in just a few years where the reality of reincarnation is demonstrated as a scientific validity. Then what we speak of will have much better appeal. Individually there is recognized tremendous knowledge already on tap. That will strengthen the right of the individual to make choice to pursue particular fields of wisdom that they might already have nurtured and want to quickly recapture.

*Do you have any ideas about how parents can be helped to get themselves to this point so that they can help the children, or will the children teach the parents?*

Both. I think you will find that the general desire that each parent carries, as far as society is concerned, is to have the best education possible. And as the value shifts as to what is the true nature of education - it is not just comparative knowledge such as testing - it will be the insight into the power of creative thinking in a variety of circumstances. And that will mean these areas that we speak of primarily now as intuitive, will be seen as valuable. The teacher and the student and the parent will be - and I use the word jokingly - co-conspirators in the process of unfolding the great adventure of knowledge that may come. And then the child will be seen as a soul old in their wisdom, and the parents more as one who helps to allow the child to find the guidance they need. There will be more friendship between children and parents, more friendship between children and teachers, less of the hard hierarchical structure. It does not mean that children will be given a broad free-for-all, but that they will rise to the level of responsibility they are allowed to achieve. And I would like to emphasize the proper phrasing of the word "responsibility," as response-to-ability.

So your question is directly, "How do you educate the teachers to educate the parents," is that not so?

220

*Yes.*

I think the common core will begin to be that there needs to be a new development of curriculum of study of insight, and teachers need to enlist the aid of the parents to some extent in the process.

*I wonder if there might be some vehicle here, like a bright idea, that could catch on of how to bring the parents around?*

I think part of it would be a watered down version of what you might term basic metaphysics. "Watered down" is perhaps inaccurate, meaning only that you would remove from it anything that might suggest a particular embodiment of belief systems that you would call cultish or guru-oriented or such as that. It would be a basic body of knowledge, beginning to be widely accepted. And the phraseology may vary a little from book to book, but you could take a selection of books that would be of value. You might take something written by someone as Mr. Leo Buscaglia and his particular passion for the right of love to flourish. That could be seen as something quite broadly acceptable. Not making him a guru, but rather, pointing to one who in their passion of insight touches deeply. So you might have a selection of such books available. One would not have to read the whole selection - they would choose from the variety. The same kinds of information would be presented, each with their particular style and flash so that they are interesting.

It would be similar to a college program in which you would say, "Here is a list of thirty books. Read three of them." You might enlist the teachers to teach the parents in such a manner. It might be a class once a week for half a semester or something to do that, you understand?

*The public school forum, then, you see as one that could*

*conceivably continue as the place for this to happen - that we begin here, and we would be able to instill all of this intuitive process in children and still maintain that as the basic forum for that to take place.*

Well, society as a whole is undergoing tremendous evolutionary pressure, tremendous change, and the educational format will not escape that, of course. It may be at times affected in the immediate moment by things such as lack of funding, but in the long run, education becomes one of the tools by which the most advanced and evolutionary processes are made known to the many. So I wish to suggest to you that the future of education is bright indeed, even if there seems to be a little darkening on the horizon just at the moment. Were you thinking of private schools as an option?

*Yes, Montessori and Waldorf have often been specifically mentioned as where education is heading, and I am wondering, will that be incorporated into the public schools?*

I think you will find definitely that those schools which are at the cutting edge of these areas of which we speak will be monitored and studied and more directly accessed in the ways that prove the value of such education. And then the techniques will begin to be integrated into the broader source of public schooling.

All that we have been speaking of lies in that realm of first being brought forth often in the private schools, but being proven as attributes, as technologies, as approaches that work. They will find their way into the schooling in the broader sense. And I think you will find also that as the shift in human awareness takes place, that education is seen as something extremely valuable, you begin to have more and more resources made available through foundations and grants and such that bring forth for the public school directly these same forms of knowledge. So it will not be only the private schooling that does the leading.

There will begin to be forms that incorporate much that the private schools now address directly. Study programs to advance the quality of teaching, programs to teach creativity, to teach intuitive, instinctual knowledge. And as the real breakthrough happens when ideas such as reincarnation, life after death, and such all become incorporated into your society as a whole. That is where the shift is so powerful that then you will see teachers elevated to a status that rightfully would be well; that they are at the leading edge of the quality control of the future.

I do not want to give you swelled heads, [laughter] but I think you can sense that education is not just of the mind intellectually. It is of the heart, the soul, the being, of yourselves and others, and that makes it a true adventure.

*In our culture we feel that many of our children do not come to school ready to learn and motivated to do so. What skills can a teacher use for classroom management techniques that would not harm the children, but let them be motivated and move into an education pattern that you described?*

In the beginning you would have to draw on the resources now readily available. If for example, there was just a bit more monies, that would be a nice start. You could have in each room a very large well-defined television situation of video-tapes and a large library available for helping to draw on the resources that are already available, such as in public televisions, into the classroom where it is appropriate, so that the teacher could interface with the curriculum those things that draw out interest. So it is a modification of the programming you now use where there is much of the book, of the reading, of the answering of questions, the written forms, the perhaps lecturing. All of that tends to be a little boring, don't you think?

So if you can sprinkle that with things that are exciting, maybe some dramatic presentations; three or four or five students take particular areas and develop a little skit; different ways to make it more exciting. All of that then begins to blossom on the basic plan that you now work with. The leaves and the structure of the trunk and all that is there now, you begin to put the blossoms, you begin to put the fruit that is sparkling, that is creative, because it draws out the interest of the students. And they might be going because they have to in the initial stage, but they begin to get excited; they begin to feel that they are truly learning something, that education can be a delightful process. It is not just killing time then. Do you understand?

*So what you are saying then, is that there would not be a problem keeping the children interested if we were to draw on all the resources that we have available already, rather than just putting them in desks, reading in certain books and doing certain papers?*

Yes. It takes time to implement this, and it does take money. I do not want to say money is the limiting factor because in a sense each teacher could in themselves find the things that are personally quite exciting and begin to dramatize in the area of their own resources those things which are exciting, and begin to build the curriculums that might take two or three years to develop and fine tune. So the amassing of the work on video would be primary, but the amassing of the resources that would be exciting in presentation can continue to take place. And you might be struggling with the limited funding. Unfortunately that seems to be the basis of education, is, "How little does it have to cost," rather than, "How could we improve it with a little more money?"

*Since money is such an issue, it seems like public relations needs*

224

*to be much greater than it is now. Do you have some thoughts about a direction for improving the image of education? How can we go about having people see the importance of it?*

Well, now you go into areas of small specifics. For example, you could begin to have one of the foundations, such as the Ford Foundation or one of the larger foundations, begin to put into the media statements such as, "Our true wealth of the nation is the breadth and the scope of education for the children." Begin to reprogram basic awareness around what education is and how valuable it is, so that then the resources begin to be made available. When bond issues come up, they do not get voted down. When the idea that the only good school is a private school developed in a particularly wealthy area, rich neighborhood, why not begin to rethink that and say, "Each school can have diversity of programming and a richness that empowers the ethnic groups that are present." So that it is not just a whitewash of cultural differences. That those cultural differences are seen as something of value and beauty that make the melting pot of your country even more valuable.

There are so many ways that the interest of the community could be triggered. And I know that as educators you struggle with that all the time. But what I am suggesting then would be what you call public relations - that there could be those companies that already have clout; they could be shifted to see the value of education. Look at your computer companies.

Look at Apple Computer for example. The vision of those who founded that corporation was that education was the primary source of future value in a culture. So there was an almost a religious imperative to spread the good word, using computers that would reach out and access the child's mind to the larger body of information available as the child was aware. They can see the

225

value of education. It not only increases the direct perception of those who might become employees, those who might develop future products, it also enhances the quality of insight in the large grouping of the public who will become future consumers. So the presentation of the educational process can begin to be seen as something that empowers everyone regardless of what they are doing. And I think that is the tack that you have to take.

Not just, "Here are these beautiful bunches of children," which is true, or, "They deserve the best," which is true. No one denies that. Everybody believes that, but to begin to reorient the mind of those in your society to see that it is important that the solidification of education be such that it is seen as a creative process; the power of the creative mind opening. So the people do not get stuck in the old thinking that all they need is the three R's [Colloquialism for: Reading, Writing and Arithmetic. Editor's note.] and that if you give them a basic education it is enough. Give them a basic education and beyond. Do not stop there. You have heard criticisms that people are in school just to learn underwater basket weaving. That is a very foolish state of consciousness. [laughter] It reflects limited, narrow thinking.

I think particularly important is that film where the man taught those in the ghetto areas advanced calculus. ["Stand and Deliver," 1988. Editor's note.] The popularity of that film points to the deep reservoir of hope in your culture that people can pull themselves out of the quagmires of limited opportunity and really find advancement. So I think inherently in your culture there is the desire that that can be so. That is what you are touching. The ways you go about touching that you have to find individually within yourselves. But I think you will find your own guidance opening insightfully to see what can be done. And then you may need to band together to start opening doors within your own communities. And if you have as an educational forum a teacher's organization,

226

you might begin to think about ways that the teacher's organization could formulate perhaps a little funding to go out and touch these companies with those large amounts of money; to do that as a public work.

Understand that in your media each station has to devote a certain amount of time to public information free of charge. You could take a company like IBM or Apple or Ford or whoever, and ask them to develop a nice little insert into your media situation that would go out and be part of the right to have valuable topics presented in your newspapers, your radios, your televisions. There are so many ways.

It seems, I know, difficult to conceive of yourself as one individual looking at the mountain of inertia that seems to be inherent around education. But remember that collectively your own instinctual self-desire goes deep into the universal consciousness and you are not alone, even if you think you are. The Spirit will work with you. Your creativity may shine, and you might even think about what other shining lights of individuality have accomplished on their own. Such as Martin Luther King - not that everyone has to become a martyr - or the woman in India [Mother Theresa. Editor's note.] who has worked with the poor there. You have examples of those, often out of a deep-seated conviction of their own Spirit about human potential.

Now I am not saying that you have to go out as a charismatic figure, but I do want you to feel that the power of your own personality is not the sole receptacle of this response-to-ability that we speak of - something that can flow through you. And it may be very subtle. It may be behind the scenes. You may never make a big flash in the public eye - or you might. But your own sense of joy about what you are doing will communicate. So rather than feeling weighted by this burden, you can find your own ways to empower yourself joyfully. That will be the biggest vehicle to allow the shift to take place that you are all desirous of. Do you understand what we mean?

*Oh yes!*

So if you are finding your body sluggish for example, and your diet is lousy, and you are wondering why you cannot make a bigger dent in the collective consciousness of the students and the parents and the academic administrators, go out and play a little golf or go swimming or go out and climb a mountain. Do something to empower the body. Your ideas will continue to bubble away. The subconscious mind will keep working with them. Inspiration will flow. Do not get stuck in your diet with a lot of stimulants that burn up the system. Try to eat a lot of food with live energy. And begin to program your own insight: As you lay down to sleep, ask that the dreams may be powerful and insightful. Write them in the morning. See what kind of creative spark they may feed you. Find fifteen minutes, half an hour a day, something of your own personal time of devotion and meditation.

Begin to enhance your ability to understand your own psychic makeup. Take some classes in healing and meditation. Take some courses in intuitive development. All of that will feed the power of that insight that you wish to impart to others. And it does not mean that you have to go about it all at once. I know that this sounds like such a huge responsibility, the way we present it. I don't want to do that. Think about it as yourself becoming young again in body, mind and Spirit. So that for you it becomes something exciting, something dramatically shifting within your own sense of what the universe can do through you.

Ultimately the ills and the problems and restrictions of the planet as you see them now serve everyone as a Divine opportunity to

228

help make change and see how unlimited the universe truly is. So that is your little pep talk!

*Great, wonderful, thank you! We need a little pep talk today. You must have known that.*

Is there one more question that anybody has?

*Well, going along with the little "pep talk," sometimes there is a big division between the people who administer the school system and the teachers. Do you have any ideas about how healing can take place and we can work together better as a whole team, as educators?*

What I would like to see, would be that there could be those who are administrating spend part of their time teaching, perhaps just assisting the teaching process. And those who are teaching could spend part of their time administrating. So that all get a better picture of the common responsibilities and desires to do what is right.

It will break down the stereotype in your society of boss and laborer. That is the movement in your field of education, as well as in your areas of business that will make the greatest impact: when everybody acknowledges that we are all in it together.

One thing I want to add. The power of prayer in individual situations might be quite significant. So if there is a situation that just feels stuck - it is in molasses, it will not move - with an individual or a group of individuals, you may individually within yourself, or collectively, if you get together two or three of you, sit down and spend five or ten minutes in focused meditation asking for healing energy to flow into that. Asking for the highest and the best of all concerned to be present.

229

If you have one in administration who seems to be stuck, be sneaky. Overshadow their stuckness with love, with compassion. And that begins to be an intangible sense of the power of the universe to start moving little mountains that seem to be in the way.

It has been our great joy to share with you.

# Meditation

*Envision yourself as a beautiful tree.*
*Rooted deep in the earth.*
*Branches in the heavens.*
*Filled with golden light.*

*The light of heaven and earth*
*course through you in communication,*
*flowing through you in balance.*

*Let there be the growing awareness*
*that you walk not alone.*

*That indeed*
*there is guidance and an opening,*
*a very personal link with the Divine*
*within you.*

*Let that be*
*what gives you the most joy in life.*

*For of all things that may be said*
*about physical existence,*
*the most singularly important process*
*you move through,*
*is your own personal link with the Divine.*
*And the awakening*
*of that universal energy.*

*That becomes the most significant*
*adventure you touch.*

*It has been our great joy to share with you.*

*Many will be the blessings*
*you will see in the years to come*
*in those areas of your endeavor.*

*God bless you.*

Chapter 16

# A Look At The Future –
# Social Issues

*God bless you.*
*It is our joy that we might share with you.*

*For each of you in your own way*
*desire to penetrate more of the awareness*
*of that indwelling place*
*that you might call the Christ or the Buddha mind.*

*To bring forth a greater sense*
*of compassion in yourself.*
*To share that with others.*

*And to move aside from the old*
*ironclad views of the past*
*that so limit humanity at this point in time.*

*To move into more of that*
*which you might call clarity*
*in the future.*

*To see the prestige energy*
*that flows through each individual*
*regardless of their calling in life,*
*how much they make in terms of monetary value,*
*or how famous they are*
*in terms of acclaim from their fellow beings.*

*For each person at the core of their Self*
*is worthy of all respect, all honor,*
*because therein lies Divinity.*

It is not so much that you have to honor the outer personality in terms of this respect, for some personalities will measure up to your standards and some will not. But if you move past the perspective of the individual as just their perspective, then you move more to the core of their being. And there can be love. There can be compassion. There can be a sense of understanding. Regardless of the machinations the personality would move through. So for some there may be deep love and compassion, and absolutely no liking. And for others there will be both, that deep sense of love and liking. The two are not synonymous.

The one in terms of liking or not liking has to do with the outer mind. The inner mind however sees through the facade of the ego. It is not caught in the illusion of suffering that the rest of humanity feels to be so, at the level of their ordinary consciousness. For the suffering is not true to the deeper part of Self. It is obviously true to the outer mind. So the question might be then, "How will we overcome this disparity?" This sense of, on the one hand, a deep cosmic union with laughter and joy and happiness; not frivolity in the sense of no serious thought, but certainly not limited by the philosophical views of the present, which somehow cast God in this old framework of a very serious being who is quick to judge.

That is not the case at all. You judge yourselves very harshly, we might add, for the most part. And if you move out of self-judgment, you will not be judging others. And conversely, if you are judging others harshly, there is a blind spot, or the mote in your own eye - that you might call a log - while trying to pick out the small speck in the other persons eye. So again, not to beat yourselves up about this, but just notice, when you grow highly critical, something in yourself is not happy with yourself.

So letting go of the former fine art of critical analysis and replacing it with an empathetic sense of, "What is within this person? What are they dealing with? What are they moving through?" Not to get lost in the association with them. Not to get lost in the empathetic bound, but to allow it to straighten out your thinking. For this is the tool of the Holy Spirit. This is the way your own deeper wisdom may function so the outer mind may learn and grow. And in that sense there are no happenstances, there are no experiences that have no value. Some obviously have more value than others, but all may reflect something of the Divine. And in the desire to share this, one with another, you will find more and more the opportunities grow and expand. And you will be given, both to yourself and others an opportunity to share. You will find ways in which the sharing may go rather deep. And this reinforces your gladness to know that you are in the body for a purpose. And the purpose is at hand.

It is to allow your light to shine. It is not about your light outshining someone else's, or that you should not be very bright because you don't want to outshine anybody. Let *all* the light shine brightly. That the darkened places in people's consciousness may be illumined. And people may be no longer afraid to stand up and take their rightful side, along with Divinity walking with them.

So in that sense you may become aware that you are the forerunners. You are like those who go out to explore before the multitudes dare think it is safe. You are those who are as pioneers, to some extent, in terms of consciousness. And if you take that pioneering Spirit, that sense of adventure in the process, you will do much to alleviate the sorrow – both of others around you and of yourself as well. For the opportunities for growth are manifesting everywhere. And where you feel guided or lead to take on a particular role or job or situation, that is also your opportunity to partake of Divine mind. To take in something of the Divine love that is your rightful heritage.

So we understand there are questionings that you may have this evening. We would be happy to focus on those or other areas of your inquiry as well.

*I would like to start with the educational field, because what you are talking about here is that..*

It is rapidly evolving.

*But it does not feel like it.*

Maybe you are expecting the results to be in the flash of a finger-snap? It takes time.

*Yes, I know I am impatient. But how are we doing?*

Well, I think you will have to break it down a bit in the growing sense of public awareness. Many people begin to see that the life-blood of any culture, any country, has to do with the young people that are growing up in that culture. For they shall be the citizens of tomorrow. They shall shape the policies and the viewpoints that you will count part of the cultural format. So the more there is a sense of the gifted, and we speak now not in terms of the few who stand out among the many, but when you think in terms of the giftedness of each child, you will see there are great recourses to be unfolded in each child.

Some will be perhaps mathematical wizards; others may like art or music. Some may combine many aspects of their seeking and their knowing. But the important thing is that they be given an opportunity to try out a variety of subject materials to see where their interest is, what they are good at. And that they are taking, of course, the observance of some of the basic programs in order to communicate better with others. But there is also a chance that they can expand past the basics, almost like you would say some are held in a kind of military environment, where they are expected to learn thus and so, no less, no more. We are speaking not of a rigid cultural standard, but now the freedom and the flexibility to help the children grow along the lines of their most strong interest - their devout sense of Self and the discovery of Self.

They will grow quickly then. And they will pick up all the other tools that are necessary as the need arises. And this is one of the areas that your Internet and your computer systems may be great facilitators in the absence of certain areas of education, where you would have experts available. You may have to rely on the technology, because there may not be that many people with expertise in the field you desire. But there will still be the need of hands-on assistance, the leadership, the guidance of the teacher, the inspiration that follows. And maybe more than one. There maybe what you term as team-teaching: two or three or even four perhaps for a larger group of children. The important thing, however, is not to burden them with excessive amounts of homework that are rote, that are drill, that are just remembering facts and figures, which is into the mind at one point, out for the testing and then promptly forgotten. It needs to be fun. And I think you will find that many people have been playing with just this type of scenario for many years now. And some are having great results. The results are not widely forthcoming in the common understanding. That is to say, these breakthroughs we speak of, have not yet hit the mainstream of public opinion. But they are moving closer. And the assistance of the Spirit is available in these endeavors if you chose to involve yourself in such a way as to make them more permanently present in you culture. Do you understand?

*Yes. But what you said about that we all need to allow ourselves and others to shine. When you work with kids, how to try to make an environment that they can shine in?*

Well, the adults need to shine a bit. Then they will pass that on to the children. When we say shine, we are not saying specifically that they should have big egos about what they are doing, but rather that they can tap into the joy and the happiness of the process. It is not so much the simple regurgitation of facts and figures and analysis based on common logic. That is almost like reading a computer program. Some of the classes may involve some of that type of thing. But there needs to be some joy, spontaneity, artistic discovery, *Self* discovery.

For example, if you were to teach the children the very simple basic steps of meditational awareness and how to ground themselves. If there is growing consciousness in your culture as to the negative effects of the drugs that are sometime administered in order to control the children, which are simply by-enlarge impacting on the children's psyche self; the structure both of the body and the emotional body; the sense of their, not Spiritual superiority, but their often strong connection with psychic awareness. This is largely misunderstood. When the diet has tremendous amounts of refined sugars, no wonder the children act up, have periodic bouts of excessive energy they don't know how to control.

So it will be more in the line of a holistic environment. Where there are those who have intuitive sight to see the energetic patterns of the children. To see those that may be more gifted in certain areas of study. And to help direct them there. So they may be more able to fulfill those areas. That is not to be exclusive, that is not to say they only get training in one area. But they may choose to exemplify those areas of interest. Learning comes quickly when what you are doing is something you are interested in. And it has a sense of enjoyment, fun and discovery. But if it is simply a re-emerging of facts and figures in order to take a test in a brilliant way, and everyone thus thinks you are smart. That has little to do with true consciousness. Do you understand?

*Yes.*

And we believe we are, you might say, speaking to the choir. That all of you are interested in the progression of humanity in different ways, particularly in educational fields. But what we are trying to impart now, is simply that with a wise use of technology, and relatively small class rooms and perhaps we should add the training for the teachers should be higher - to a higher standard and thus compensation as well. Not that you have to pour money into things to make them function, but if people are forced to hire themselves out in a part time job to make ends meet, it gives them little time for resourcing the material that may be that which the children would enjoy. Do you understand?

*I think so.*

Simply put, where there is enough income to function easily in the society, the teachers that are truly interested in teaching will spend some of their research-time on things that will function for the individual students. Not all students are the same. You have to be open to your own guidance and inspiration when you are in the position of teaching.

*So are you saying more teachers and smaller classes?*

More appreciation for the value of what the teachers are helping to impart.

For the crossroad of society is such that those who would build a better society will start with the children. And who then is the most responsible for that role? It is those who function well in the given environment of teaching, not of mass amounts of students, rolling

240

through some kind of production line. You can have certain amounts of teaching that value the basic subjects. But if that is all there is, it is rather boring for most students. And when things are boring, they don't learn. So there needs to be a variety of approaches. To format that which would work with one child, may not with another. There needs to be a sense of flexibility therefore. And what we are trying to impart is not just a sense of a strongly academic education. This may fill the head with facts and figures, but it does not give much in the way of response to the true joy of learning, the true joy of self-discovery. So it needs to be an artistic, holistic environment.

All those areas have value, depending on the student and their particular frame of reference. And one year a very strongly interested child, may pick one area and focus individually on that to a great extend. And then a year or two later it may be something else, and then maybe three or four years later it might be a whole range of subjects, because there is then seen more the interlinking of knowledge.

True knowledge supersedes classifications. It is not caught in a particular discipline. It is widely available through a variety of disciplines. And that is the beauty of the educational process for all of humanity: to discover new avenues of Self-awareness, to discover that you have doorways to the Soul you did not even know you had. So we would wisely say that those who are interested most truly, and believing in their own self-worth, they will help impart that to others. And there will be those whose strong desire and strong motivation, is to help with the children in such an endeavor.

Whether young or old, the chronological age is still not the essence of the process. You can be a hundred and twenty five years old - or whatever would pass for old age - and still be a child in your learning process. So it is that spark of adventure we speak of now. Whether young in the body or old in the body. The inner child is worthy of an adventuresome life, an admiration for the value and the skills that may be gathered, but most of all not to be based on just a simple monetary analysis. If you simply value people by how much they can produce, how much they make, then the society is heading in the wrong direction. Don't you think?

*Yes.*

Perhaps that is not the particular form of the question you had in mind, but we would be happy to pursue whatever you would like to deal with a bit further.

*What you have been saying here is our goal, but are we heading in that direction? Because here in the US right now, under this government, the quality measurement of education has been reduced to testing and grades.*

That will be short lived. Don't get caught in the little bumps in the road; the momentary ups and downs of quality of environment in your educational process. In the long run you begin to see as a collective - across the planet, not just in one culture, but the whole of the human race - you begin to see the emergence of highly skilled individuals at a very young age. You start to value the remarkable ability to comprehend, that this so-called young child may have, in advance of those even who may be their teachers. More and more there are old souls being born. Young in body, but not in Spirit. And the knowledge they seek, they have already grasped to a large extent. They want to get through the basic process and go on. And their skills will come forward in every adventure of human endeavor. In every field there will be those advanced in their wisdom. But most of all they will come to bring forth the joy of human endeavor. Not just in one area, but in all

242

areas. The joy will predominate.

We are speaking of the next twenty, thirty, perhaps even fifty of your years. It has to be seen in the broad span of time. The momentary ups and downs are a bit like the waves on the ocean. The ocean still functions. If the waves are great or they are quiet and flaccid, there is still this vast body of water. And the analogy might be made: there is within each person a vast awareness from the domain of Spirit, waiting to be represented in the daily consciousness. And it is beginning to tap that resource, that will change the face of education, as you know it.

It will also change the face of human experience on planet earth. No longer will governments be permitted to stand by in ignorance where there is a need of human compassion. It will be an integration; the highest aspects, the art, the music, all the elements that make up a society in a positive sense, will be brought forward to be honored more directly. This will come. We are looking at a twenty to a twenty-five years scenario from present time now.

Shall we continue?

*Will we ever learn to choose leaders with insight and wisdom?*

Well, you are learning that in a negative sense at the moment. We are teasing you a little bit.

*Could it be that if we have a president who is not coming from insight and wisdom, and who speaks a lot war and fear, could it be that the people might grow more insightful and wiser because of the lack of it in the leadership?*

No, not specifically now to speak of your political environment, but perhaps we must say this to clarify the issue: There is within each person a place of greater clarity and a place of fear. Collectively it might be a scene as though the wind were blowing over a deck of cards; they all seem to fall in the same direction. But ultimately, no one will take the word from someone else as to what is true. They will begin to feel from within themselves. From within the depth of their own knowingness. And this shall be the salvation of society and cultures everywhere. That as human wisdom advances, and individuals grow collectively more attuned to Spiritual realities. And then they will cease to function in the patterns of fear that someone may bring forth as a political leader.

Once people stop listening to the politics of the day and start looking at the inner wisdom or the like thereof, whether it is present or not present, they will start to see the individuals in question in terms of: "Are they truly able to be Divinely guided? - to be touched by the Spirit?" so to speak. And we are not speaking now of necessarily someone highly intuitive in the obvious sense, but those that are well grounded, well balanced and have a measure of success in the attitudes of releasing their own fear patterns. So they don't respond in fear if there is an attack or a seemingly disastrous event taking place. They would not necessarily gloss it over. We are not saying that. But they may come about with a more creative solution that draws upon the courage and the admirable traits in each person to help resolve the situation. Rather than in fear - defense and attack - that is the commonality of the human ego everywhere. Once you master that which you can step beyond; simple attitudes of fear, patterns of defense and attack, you will begin to see there are those with remarkably clear judgment. Those are then to be the leaders. So in the present society you might say it is the darkness before the dawn.

*And isn't that just necessary?*

It is a part of the pattern, a part of the evolution of the species. A

244

bit like a swinging pendulum; you get some keen insights and you listen to others, and you hear all the fear and then you start to question: "What about these insights – were they real or not?" And then you start to see what the fear brings about, what it manifests. And then you might say something to the effect: "Well, I don't care whether the fear is real or not, I am going to listen to my heart. I am going to do the things that I feel are best for all of humanity. Not just caught in my own selfish little world, based on fear patterns." And when people start to do that, things shift, the patterns change. Healing in essence takes place among the whole of the human race. For all the fear and anxiety that may be forth coming at the moment, ultimately, it is just not so. It is not the true reality at all.

The ego would feel shattered to embrace the depth of the Divine. So it gets it in small doses. A bit like the two-step dance; two steps forward, one step back. In time, the ego will welcome the release from the desire and the acceptance of fear as a reality. It will step into a greater cognizance of love. And in that form the ego is transformed, out of patterns of fear into a delight in the light; a delight in the human observance of Spirit flowing everywhere. Available to all people, regardless of their need. This is like breathing oxygen. You would think it very strange to be on a planet with no oxygen. In time you will feel very strange if anybody cannot have clarity of heart. It will be like they stopped breathing. They chose to become mummified. They chose to become as dead while still in the body.

But until that takes place - and mind you there is no force in this - there is no effort by God to say, "All those who do not listen to my words will be challenged to throw themselves into some pit of fear or fire – *not true*." Divinity calls forth only the blessing in each individual. It is they themselves who fight the allowance of whether or not they will receive the blessing. The Universe just chuckles and waits. If they are not ready now, give them a few millennia. [Laughter] We tease you a bit now.

*So could we say in the future that there might not be one political leader or one religious leader, but that it would be the one and same?*

You will have those who you admire greatly and respect, who will be in a sense the spokes-person for the vast majority of people. But you will not be so prone to put your religious and you Spiritual leaders on pedestals. You will see they have particular brands of skill, particular areas of knowledge. And they function best when given some sense of freedom to work in those areas. But they are not meant to be as dictators, and certainly not to be necessarily a guru of all people. The master Jesus came forth many, many years ago saying: "These are the things that are true for you, as well as for me." But of course, society was not ready to hear that. In time now, your society will be quite generally ready to hear the message of truth in whatever words it would flow in, that they may receive. It is still in its essence the same message. Not a different message, but the same. Though called by various names, still it is one and the same, ultimately.

Yes, you have more questioning?

*Just a quick question so I get it. Is it maybe so that we are going to be our own leaders, and that people are going to be more equal in that sense? So people are not just following one leader, but gaining their individual power back?*

I think you will as a human race, come to understand that when leadership causes fear, they are no longer in a position of leadership. Where there is hatred, where there is anxiety, where there is fear based thinking, that no longer is acceptable as people begin to awaken.

Many people will awaken simultaneously at one point in time. You might call it a "big bang." [Laughter] We are teasing you just a little bit. But relatively speaking, that is so in terms of relative time. It does not take a lot of people to become fully conscious, to affect the whole. The patterns of a few might have great power to abundantly catalyze the action of others into deeper modes of thinking and feeling.

*So if I can just ask about one of the "bumps in the road," as you termed them earlier. Because it feels important and stirs up a lot of emotions in this country right now: The presidential election is coming up and the opponent to the standing president seem more mature and openhearted in his approach, but still he also has this big focus on terrorism and all the fear around that.*

Well, people are not quite ready to let go of their fears yet. So if he was to bandy it about, that he is actually in favor of trade with the terrorists, you can imagine what an uproar that would bring about. We are not saying that he is, but we are simply using an extreme example of, "Oh, lets make friends with the terrorists, they are hungry, they are cold, they are bitter. Give them some sugar for their coffee." We are teasing you now.

Just the whole point of view of the terrorists versus those that are not feeling safe, is simply that the terrorists have won when people don't feel safe. That is the whole point of being a terrorist. When you begin to see people unafraid, without fear. Then they cannot be terrorized. So it is a wake up call for the whole of the human race to begin to root out fear wherever it exists within the self. It is not "out there" to go off and kill the bad guys, you understand? It is out there in the sense that the objective mind, the analytical, personal view will be saying, "There is something out there that I

247

should fear, something I should protect myself from." And then to go a bit deeper in analysis and step into the greater mind and think, "Oh no, this is not so. There is no reason for fear. Even if I drop the body, there is still no reason for fear. Even if my children and my families are threatened, there is still no reason for fear." That is a bit of a stretch, you understand?

*Yes.*

Nobody in their so-called "right mind," in your culture at present time, will think to call that some kind of informed thinking. But if you see from the eyes of your Soul, then you don't have to worry about convincing yourself of the truth of what we have just spoken of. If you see from the eyes of yourself as an eternal being, which you are, then you will realize, "Well, all that is lacking is the depth of true love." Purpose-full-ness - the adventure of helping to shift consciousness - is an aspect of the joining of the union with Divine mind and your culture, your consciousness, your position, your society. It functions in all areas. It will bring about a gentle transformation of the fear into a fearlessness. With fearlessness, with courage, you move forward, you begin to accept the norm in other cultures for what it is. Sometimes more enlightened, sometimes not so. And where there is the assistance that may be given, you go forward to give it. So then the world becomes a stage for the enlightenment opportunity. It is not just one culture.

Perhaps we have gotten a bit too broad with the answer to your question. But in order to respond we must suggest that if you have, on the one hand Mister Bush and on the other hand Mister Kerry, if one of them would come too far forward, in a sense of fearlessness – at this point in time – they would not get elected. So the old adage that someone can play on fear, still hold sway. But humanity will outgrow this. It is an old pattern. That is what you are seeing now, is the struggle between the more enlightened stages of human

248

growth and development, and old patterns of thought that are ready to be tossed into the trash.

Let us continue.

*This question is about families and relationships. There are a lot of divorces happening at time being and people are getting together in a different way, with different people, in different family settings. I am just wondering if this expanded family structure we are seeing now, is part of the human experience of that we are all "one big family?"*

You have seen the patterns of more and more the eradication of fear. One of the strongest fears is not belonging, not being part of the group, not being able to join. So the smallest pattern is often the family structure where one has some sense of belonging, even if not feeling too competent to be part of the larger culture. But even as you say, it is so. That humans begin to aspire for a larger family environment unconsciously. They begin to desire the ability to step past the bonds of love limited by genetic transference - the human genes everyone is so concerned about. At some point in human history, all of this was relevant and important to some extent. But now you don't find yourself crossing off long lists of the prospective bride or groom, depending on their previous history as a family. That may still have some importance in areas of nobility and the function of how arrangements are made for the partnership, but even that is changing. What we are saying is that you don't look at your prospective partner the way you would look at the lineage of a racehorse. Bloodlines and all of that become unimportant.

And when you begin to sense that not only genetically are you stepping back and re-thinking the whole process in terms of the politics of, "Who has the best genes?" [Laughter] We are teasing

249

you a little now. You are beginning to think, "O, my gosh, have I known this person in other lifetimes? What was the relationship like then? How well did we get along? Will we be able to master life's sorrows and the events that may seem negative, and allow the joy to come forth? Are we truly representative, one for another, of a Divine opportunity for growth?"

Then you have a remarkable process stepping up. It is like a new batter to the plate - a new game about to begin. [As in baseball. Editor's note] Humanity about to strike a home run in order to succeed where there has been not so much success in the past. So you may find every form of love available in terms of family structure; some will choose not to marry, some will marry for life, those that may have many partners.

But the common bond will be the *authenticity* of the love involved. You have the capacity to love everyone on the planet. And we are not speaking now romantically, but in terms of your subjective self. The knowingness that is carried deep within you of the Divine energy each person carries, makes them completely lovable. Divinity loves you in a fashion far beyond any language to express. There are no components in your experience as a human being that we can use to help quantify the power of Divine love that moves through you even now, and always shall and always has.

So the human experience is one of an awakening that is relatively slow by the standards of planet Earth. It is very quick in terms of that which is the ultimate awareness, for time moves quickly now and you begin to wake up as a planet. You begin to shift in terms of your own sense of inner worth. You begin to feel the lifelong opportunity there to engage in Divine drama, rather than human drama. So your patterns is shifting: Maybe you wanted sweet stuff as a child - pickles, ice cream, candy bars, etc, lots of snacks - and then you get a little older and you discover *really good food*, with life force in it. It is a bit like that. You are beginning to wake up collectively to realize you want the quality of relationship to manifest.

That means honesty of communication. That may mean some treatment toward the skills of lovemaking, that would be something studied and understood: The mechanism of the human body, both the male and the female, in terms of the energetic exchange that is possible. Not just the mighty climax. Not just looking at the human anatomy in terms of, "What is the greatest turn on?" There are people who make that a life study, but experience little if any love in the process.

We are speaking now of the eradication of fear in the field of lovemaking, which would mean clear communication. It would mean communication first of all with Self: "As Self – what do I truly want to experience? What do I want to share? How deeply can I go in the feeling of love with another? It is basically to the degree that I love myself. If I do not love myself, another may shower me with love, and I will not be able to take it in." It is that kind of realization that begins to transform relationships at every level. And then what will be strangely interesting is that sexuality in and of itself will become less important.

Humanity will begin to awaken to the vast blossoming of love with Divinity, *shared* with another individual. It is like, rather than worrying over one cut rose you have got sitting in your living room, in this beautiful vase, and the pedals fall off and you start to panic, "I am loosing my rose. The bloom of youth is gone. I will no longer be attractive to anyone." You see the analogy? And then you step out the door and you find that you are surrounded by a field of the most beautiful roses producing colors and vibrations of energy in every form. That is a bit as though you step past the fear of romance or the addiction, shall we say, to physical romance.

251

And you suddenly start to embrace the Divine romance. And this, in all likelihood, you may choose to share with one individual. Not to make a mockery of the sexes, because you can enjoy lovemaking with many people, that is not the point, it is more the quality of the heart that begins to come forth in every form of relationship. And in that you find that you can go very deep, particularly in the skills of advanced healing work; in counseling, in creativity, in those things which are non-fear based. Perhaps you sit down to write a novel. And you get deep into it. And you start to find that the characters take on their own personalities. They start to write themselves. And you are almost just a witness to the process and it leaves you with this feeling of immense gratitude to be able to produce something of that nature.

Because the creative energy flowing through you is its own reward. We are not addressing now the factors of publicity in printing and publications, and all the monies, and all that that's involved with. We are speaking of the actual energy of creative expression. If you are teaching others, you may constantly worry, "Am I doing a good enough job? Shall I put out more advertising? Should I have talked to so and so, because perhaps they are ready?" You see the patterns? All the questions that may enter the ordinary mind? But when you relax into it and you feel; "Divine mind has a hand in this process. Those people that need to be here, are here. I did what I could on the physical level, but most of all I am glad to share the energy with all these wonderful people."

And the expression of love through you, takes its own form, and the fears drop away. The personality consequences, the views, the analysis, the agonizing over choices you have made - all that falls away. And the joy in Divinity expressing itself, being received and reverberated through the group. It is as so each one takes it in and broadcasts it back, takes it in and broadcasts it back. It gets stronger and stronger. And miracles take place.

That is the nature of the next step in human evolution. It is beginning to embrace the potential, miraculous happenings, to help you understand you are no longer limited by yourself, conceived of as a physical being. You have a body - you have a wonderful vehicle, but you are Soul. You are Spirit. You are this ageless being waking up in the fullness of human consciousness as an expression of the Divine. That is the full measure of family and relationship at every level, as you begin to feel how deeply Divinity loves you. And loves everyone through you. You are then in *awe* of your true nature.

Perhaps we should not hold the body too much longer.

# Meditation

*If you will hold now*
*just a little time of quietude.*

*Go just a little deeper.*

*Each of you feeling your way*
*into the very heart of the planet.*

*Feeling the earth as mother.*
*The surrounding trees,*
*the mountains,*
*all that you find in abundance*
*on the planet*
*as part of your own being.*

*As so your fingers, your toes,*
*your thoughts, reach out,*
*begin to embrace the immensity*
*of Divine mind in deep personal contact*
*with you.*

*It has been our great joy to share.*
*Good evening and God bless you.*

Chapter 17

# Timeless Thoughts
# For The Modern Mind

*God bless you.*
*It is indeed our joy*
*that we might share with you.*

*For each of you in your own way*
*find a growing sense*
*of clarity from deep within Self.*

*And you may at times feel*
*as though you are battling just a bit*
*with the ego*
*trying to take charge again and again.*

*But we would assure you*
*that you are simply letting go,*
*more and more,*
*of the ego's predisposition*
*toward trying to control*
*your awareness of yourself.*

*And as that ego control slips,*
*what begins to emerge*
*is a greater contact*
*with the deeper wisdom that is natural,*
*that is native to your being.*

You have within you countless incarnations of insight that have been built before this time in the body. Not all of that of course will be clearly remembered, but still the essence of change that you seek to accomplish has already been done in many other lifetimes. So it is not a new thing, it is not a difficult thing to let go of the past in the sense of what angers you or upsets you or causes you to doubt the beauty that you carry. Letting go of those types of traumatic events, or subtle layers of programming by the culture, or by your birth process, or by remembered experiences of other lifetimes that might be considered as negative. Letting *all* of that go is truly a step in the right direction. It is not throwing away the learning that may have come from that, but it is letting go of the doubt, the guilt, the fear, the anxiety, the sense of not being worthy of Divine love.

For almost without any language to express, the reality of love is far greater than what could be spoken of. It is a measure of observation, when you feel at times sweeping over you a profound love of nature, for the earth, for animals. Sometimes for the beauty of a sunset or perhaps a piece of music you have listen to, or a particularly deep friendship, where you may have had a clear discussion of attitudes and insights shared. Those feelings are rooted deep within your own being and they are the hallmark of trust in the nature of the Divine Mind that would function with you and through you. We want to emphasize both, because when it is with you, you get a sense of the camaraderie, the friendship of the Divine, chuckling with you, showing you new insights, and never judging in the sense of the harshness of the ego's judgment. Always reminding you that you are created out of the Divine matrix. You are created out of Divine awareness. That is the essence of your being.

To the level of which you might express the energy through you as a vehicle, you might call it a kind of channeling process. It certainly does not need to be in a trance state. But it might be a moment of inspiration or creative insight. Like a particularly clear dream or a deep conversation with another. Or perhaps you are writing a letter to someone and you show your heart; you let out what you feel. And perhaps you have insight into their process, that you are speaking to, which you may or may not be aware of. Because the channeling process may evoke your insight or it may flow past it. So that there is a sense of saying something or writing something, and you are not quite sure why that felt so important. But it was. And it was important in that it communicates to the other individual some of *their* key insights that they are ready to receive.

So you might say that life is this wonderful mix of deepening awareness of yourself, for yourself. And sharing the loving energy, the compassion, with others, in which insight is also linked. It is like the weaving of cloth. You have two different directions the cloth is woven in. And through life, the compassion is woven perhaps behind your vision, but still it is there. It is woven into all that you say and do ultimately. Though at times you may wonder where Divinity has gone. It is only that the ego has stepped aside from that knowledge. Not that Divinity has ever moved. For the changeless does not change. Divinity is beyond the effect of the ego's experience, but it is not beyond the ability to transform the ego when you are willing, when you will allow it.

So in the history of human events, you may always find certain elements of dramatic experience, the ego having it's way for a time. If you want to look at history as often it is seen, in wars and rebellions and uprisings, one might wonder, "What in the world is humanity doing to enjoy the privilege of being born into the body, and then misusing that gift so dramatically?" And we would remind you that through all of this, the hunger of the soul to experience the Divine is still intact. Eventually individuals, who have been through wars, get tired of it. And they stop doing that. It is like a child playing in the sand box, perhaps a bit as though you would knock over the other persons sand castle. Eventually that gets boring.

So it is that mankind grows through both positive and negative experiences. But the quicker one is when your own self realizes what the motivating factor is. It is your deep and abiding hunger for Divine contact that moves underneath the surface of all things you seek. Every form of an addiction, underneath that addiction there is still the desire for Divine contact. Perhaps one goes about it in completely the wrong way, but that lesson will give a lasting direction later on, to move in the right way. So rather than judge yourself too harshly, allow yourself the ability to back up from a previous point of believe or conception and take another look: What was the situation in its essence? What were you hungry for? What was the other person or persons hungry for? And if you look at something so extremely negative as the holocaust in World War Two, you may think, "How could it possible be so? That Hitler has an ounce of Divinity shining somewhere?" And we would say, "Remember that no one dies." We are not condoning any act of violence, but no one dies.

When those who have perpetuated such atrocities come to the realization of what they have done, they are truly the ones in need of the healing. So let the compassion grow rich and deep in spite of all the obstacles that seem to be present in the broad spectrum of human experience. All it takes is one individual to dive deep enough inside to touch the Divine in full measure. And that individual will awaken to a Presence so profound that the world itself is changed. You have history of those individuals in some remarkable examples such as Jesus or Gandhi or Mother Theresa or many others. But there are countless numbers of awakening souls who also affect the balance. They bring about a shift in consciousness and though they may not be note worthy in the eyes of the world in the moment of their living, still the effect continues to grow. And if they are no longer in the body, still from the realm of Spirit, that effect continues to function.

For the power of the Divine just magnifies all the love that is present in each person, to remind them that their own Divinity lies complete and whole and is intact; has never disappeared, has never gone anywhere. So the function of divorcing yourself from the past is not to try to hide it. It is simply to let it go. Let the perfection of Divine mind shape and mold you into the qualities, which are already aligned with your own deep desire. Of that you need have no fear. And as Divinity awakens within each individual, the shifting patterns of the whole of humanity move also in that direction. You have at this time very old souls entering the body in the form of your young children. It will be very quick that mankind begins to express levels of consciousness that in the past, even as recently as two- or three hundred of your years, those insights would have been considered almost as a miraculous event. They will become more commonplace. That which is miraculous however will continue to unfold: That you will see in the twinkling of an eye, ailments healed. You will see people long bothered by thought processes, which are suicidal or extremely negative, suddenly brought about to be in a balance, where they realize they have been missing the key component of their own knowing, which is their foundation in love.

All of this we may talk about intellectually, but what we are actually speaking of now, is a shift in consciousness. It is not just an intellectual probing that brings about this shift in consciousness, it is a willingness to go deep within the Self and uncover that beautiful light that lies there. To let it shine forth and to not be frightened that somehow your ego thinks it needs to take credit for the miraculous events that will follow. The true miracle always makes itself clearly known that it was devoid of the contamination of the ego. The ego may step back in wonderment and than step forward and say, "Look what I did." But all the time there is this big chuckle. You actually did nothing. All you did was step aside and allow the power of the Divine to function in its rightful way.

The ego has the ability to be transformed into the awareness that you have gathered through many incarnations of your unique individuality. That is the true gift. The ego was in a sense designed to be the custodian of too much memory, so you would not remember all the lifetimes you have spent in Divine service. You would not remember how long you have hungered for Divinity. You would not remember the times when you where forgetful and thought you where somehow separate from the Divine. And all manner of things you call bad took place. All of these things the ego was designed to shield you from, while you chose to experience the individualization process. But now that cycle is coming to its conclusion. Individuality has been safely developed now, it is time to go on and allow the fulfillment of that pattern which no longer needs to establish itself as a barrier to your remembrance. The ego's power to control is shifting rapidly into a place of observance, a witness, and the more you allow yourself to witness the flow of energy that you may be part of, the more you allow yourself to step aside and allow the Spirit to function with you and through you. The more you will be reminded of the immense love the universe holds for each person and the perfection that they *do* exist in.

In that way you will come to see all of life as a gift unto yourself. The experience you have brought forward is one of deep choice. Patterns before this life have been planned. Patterns have been planned with other people, some you would meet in the body, some you would work with in the Spirit, some you have yet to meet. But still the planning is one of mutual expression of Divine

260

mind functioning with you and through you. So now is the time of the great homecoming, the time of remembrance that is beginning to sweep across the planet, as you would view the wind moving the fields of wheat ripe for harvest. As you would see the flicker of the waves upon the ocean, reminding you that there is this awakening that you are part of, that others are also ready for. But most of all, Divinity is also hungering to allow you that privileged of your awakening.

You are not being forced into this in any artificial sense, it is as though finally you hear the calling and respond. It is just that simple.

So in remembrance of all you have done before, if memories come forward you don't like, do not worry. There are those memories which are even more threatening to the ego, because you have been so magnificent. Those are the ones most difficult to allow to come forward. You will not challenge yourself to become an inflated ego because of Spiritual remembrance. Quite the opposite. You will stand in *awe* of the beauty that may present itself through you or any other individual. The things that the Master was able to do, that He said quite clearly, "These that I do, ye shall do, and even grater." That promise still stands.

In conclusion: Remember Divinity *longs* to wake up with you in your own consciousness. It has always been present. But the gift of sharing is an immense joy. The Universe awaits your awakening by your own willingness to allow it to be so.

Let us then look upon the questionings you may have at this point in your own thought process.

*Will every rock and every stone also be reset into a higher vibration? In my musings it seems like our planet will be reset.*

261

You are speaking now of the removal of toxins and things out of the atmosphere and the waters?

*I was thinking of a quickening, like moving from a third dimension into a fifth dimension or something like that.*

Well, those may be ways of trying to speak of this transformation that we are referring to. The language may be used of course in different ways, but the important thing to remember is that the world is as a thought in the mind of God. And as people begin to awaken, they more directly penetrate into that experience of the thought process - for want of better words to express what we are trying to say. That thought process that under-girds all of existence, and there you realize there is nothing, to use your slang; "Cast in stone." There is nothing that is without the ability to be transformed. So you might say that planet earth now functions as a radically clear vehicle through which human experience may be earned in the away of choice to make that experience. But in time you will simply upgrade, as though moving from your grade in your schooling to another. So I think the analogy holds true. How you choose to express it, the language particularly when it is extremely poetic, would try to express the thought that as when the Master Jesus walked into the hallelujahs and the wonderment of the people, [Reference to His triumphant entrance into Jerusalem. Editors note.] and he said if they did not bring praises, then the very stones would do so. He was speaking of the triumphant awakening of consciousness that transforms perception of all things. So perception changes, and when perception changes, the reality of what you experience is definitely different. It cannot be the same.

They are beginning to look upon the discoveries of the scientists of today and realize there is nothing physical. What a monumental insight. Which the mystics have talked about down through the pages of all histories. So I think you have the right of it, however you would like to express it. Do you understand?

*Thank you. How long will it be before we really will be using alternative energies versus...*

Well, it is a question about what you mean by really. But it is moving more in that direction. In the next twenty-five to thirty-five, perhaps forty of your years, you will probably derive perhaps a maximum of at least half of the energy usage from such endeavor. And it will rapidly shift as the recommended insight is such that the use of oil and other attributes stored in the earth from the past will be seen to be used more for the manufacturing process of new... I don't think you would call them plastics. But there will be many things that will be more available to you through the utilization of coal and oil, not for burning, not for the heat value, but rather for the resources of which manufacturing can take the use of these things. Do you understand?

*Yes.*

And you will use sun; you will use the solar energies and the wind energies. And you will perhaps in time find the focus of broadcasting these energies over great distances, without wires. But that is a bit premature to speak of in the moment. Some of these technologies you have had in the past, in the time of Atlantian cultures, and they will begin to be rediscovered too. But perhaps not too quickly. For more important than the technological development, is the shift in human consciousness. And when mankind awakens fully to the awareness of the power of love, then the technological developments will be just as tools to support that love. Do you understand?

*Great. Okay. Thank you.*

Other questionings, comments or insights?

*What you are saying now makes me relieved, because there are so many people having this feeling that the earth is still in the danger zone. That we are going to...*

Blow up the planet?

*Right, and there is this specific fear, like in the Mayan calendar about the year 2012...*

I think that is symbolic of a point in time where human history steps out of the old patterns into a new level of consciousness. And you cannot say precisely this second, this moment, this hour, this day that this will happen. But as humanity begins to awaken, the shift will be rather rapid. It is as though once established, the reality of Spiritual dimensions beyond the physical, the world as you know it begins to change. It is already happening in the minds and hearts of many, but once – perhaps you say – it gets into the Millennian consciousness; science for example begins to build upon the principals of the Almighty, the Divine inherent in every fiber of creation. The language may not necessarily be presented in religious terms, but it will still express an underlying development of patterns of insight that are harmonious, that are clearly designed *in* the thought of something much more majestic than human history has alluded to in the past.

People will begin to wake up on a very broad scale. And I think that 2012 may be for some quite a fearful time because we would remind you, without a doubt, the ego fears above all else a Spiritual awakening. For it believes, it *absolutely* believes, that it will die as that takes place. So many of the writings and books and forecasts and prophecies you may hear about that seem to be fear based, are strictly speaking, the ego's last dying effort to convince you not to go there. Because it is afraid it will die. And it will.

In the collective sense the ego will die to the patterns of the past: the judgments, the jealousies, the quickness to anger, the quickness to defense. All of that which the ego has mastered as a way of defending itself, to rely upon itself, to be in control - will slip. And suddenly that which you call the ego will have a transformation, will be given new levels of responsibility, as an individualizing function to allow the individual to begin to merge with the Divine Whole.

The completeness of the cycle will take place. But it is not as though your individuality will be lost, it is just that the ego - as it understands itself - that will be gone. So from the ego perspective at present time it is definitely fearful. From the perspective of what *will be then*, the radical transformation then begins to move quickly throughout your global affairs, your economics, your political events, your relationships – one with another. Your understanding of the past and of the future. Your understanding of time. And perhaps much more rapidly the guidance will open to receive the abundance of welcoming knowledge of others from other dimensions of consciousness that you might refer to as Spirit. And also others from states of physical consciousness in other places in the galaxy. All of this is still in the awareness of Divine mind. It is not as though you step into special categories. This all exists. It has always existed. It is just that humanity begins to awaken to it.

So we would say: Let not fear, whether your own or the fear that others may focus upon, fool you into thinking that somehow the world is going to come to a screeching halt. This the ego does believe, but it is absolutely false. Do you understand?

*Yes.*

Shall we continue? Are there other questionings?

*Does that mean that the purpose of the ego will end?*

Well, the purpose of the ego will end, as the ego has understood its purpose. But it will not end in the sense that there will be no need for it. You are not going to just dissolve into some kind of cosmic bliss. There will still be work to be done. There will still be pockets of awareness in individuals scattered around the globe, who are not ready to wake up yet. And they have that right. No one is forced into an awakening. But there will be then, let us call it the romantic ideal of fathoming the guilt, the fear, the doubt, so well that it dissolves. It is gone. It is history. It no longer exists. In fact, it will be understood at that point in awareness to have never existed. It is like the memory of a bad dream, and you awaken, and you know it was false, it was not real. And in that point the ego is radically transformed. You can call it by whatever name you want: Enlightenment, the awakening of the Heart, the Christ consciousness being born, the second coming, the birth of Divinity within, new wine - understanding from your scriptures - you have the ability to be born in consciousness again. And that is what we are speaking of.

So your beautiful uniqueness will be radiantly present. There will just be more joy. For example, if you meet a friend, there is now for most of you, this secret little exiting expectation, "Oh, here is someone possibly I have known before. Possibly there is the capacity for deepening of friendship. Possibly we might reveal something one to another of the beauty that we are afraid to admit to, but we know is present." As that shift becomes more powerful, it will not be just a slight little possibility, it will be an absolute reality.

This is what normally takes place when people who are aware

266

meet one another. They understand the inner workings of the other. And they are open as though they are transparent, that the other may see the inner workings of the heart, and all is reinforced in the joy. We always like to tease and say Jesus and Buddha hang out in the same bar in heaven. It is a very subtle way to suggest that they have *no conflict* over the states of consciousness they carry. Now, if you get a very typically good Christian and typically good Buddhist together, they might get stuck on the differences of approach, and the details, the language, the various forms of meditation and prayer. And the expectations of what heaven is about. And a belief in a deity or a non-deity etc, etc. That is human consciousness trying to decide what Divinity is about. But when you experience the Divine, you don't have to have an argument over who is right. You share the experience. So that is the kind of an awakening that the ego will be transformed into. Do you understand?

*Yes. I have a follow-up question to this, because I am thinking about my own background. I have my specific training in the alternative health field, and for a while during my training I thought that that was the only way. I am realizing that it is not so, but many of us, even in the alternative field, are still saying that, "Mine is the one way."*

Well, this will remain until the mind is completely merged into the process of, I don't want to use the word association, it is as though the mind of the heart, the mind of the soul, the mind of Divinity itself, become united. And therein no longer are you measuring experience in forms of theoretical knowledge – beliefs about experience. These may vary. Individuals will each carry their own brand of reflective thought of what reality is to them. And that may change, but there is still that anchoring in the belief about what reality is. *But* when you are in reality, you don't have to construct or support or feel attached to, anything other than the truth itself.

And that truth truly allows you freedom.

It is not about one person's brand of heaven being better than another's. You take joy in the sharing and the co-creativity, and the Spirit of insight that may flow. People will still find amazing powers of love awakening in them, particularly in the need that someone else may have. If someone is still troubled, there is some resistance, their need will draw through you more of the miraculous. So think not that, perhaps in fifty or one hundred years from now, you find yourself in Spirit and you think, "Well, what then will I do? What good will be healing? What good will be prophecy? What good will be clairvoyance? What good will it do to shape a pot on the potters wheel?" All of these things which give richness of experience, will be with you.

And the extension of that richness, of that love, will find just a more profound capacity to function. The periodic doubt that may creep into the mind now, "Perhaps I am not really doing God's will?" will be replaced with a sense of, "God's will lies before me and I walk into it gladly and abide in the privilege of that process. And I remain in that process, whatever it would bring."

The trust becomes cemented. The details of life that are so agonizingly thought through now, will be no longer such. You will not struggle with choices. You will flow with the insight of your deepest desire and allow that to guide you. And let us make clear that we are not speaking of just some point in the future when you are no longer bound by a physical body. That state of awareness may be fully present now, in the body. And so much greater then is the joy when you have mastered the awakening that allows you to feel that heavenly consciousness being part of you, while you are yet in the body.

Because while you are in the body, it is like a lever: You can shift energy more powerfully for other people when you are in the body and they are in the body. Don't know if we can make a clear analogy with that. It is a bit like a transformer. If you take the electricity you use in you home, it has to be brought down in voltage. It is far too high a voltage as it traverses the wires across vast distances. Something of that might be said, that while you are in Spirit, you can functions with very high voltages, but to step them down so they have usefulness in the physical dimension. There is the need of some form of physical contact, a transforming process. And when you are in the body and you awaken, you become a transformer. Sounds a bit crude, but it is a good analogy, we think at the moment at least. Perhaps we will come up with something better.

*I have another question. About three or four years ago, at one of the Easter seminars, there was a man who had developed this, it was like, high oxygen or something, but he dropped these tablets into a bay that was dead, was polluted, and the whole thing got cleaned up and brought back to life. It was just amazing. I just wonder if we will reach a point, I mean I feel that the inventions are out there, but will humanity embrace the cleaning up of the oceans?*

Oh, I think once people begin to awaken, all manner of technologies will step forward to assist in the process. As again, we have already suggested, the world is just an idea in the mind of the Divine. And finding the balance, to find the clarifying of the airs, the removal of toxins, the industrial waste products, all these things may seem insurmountable obstacles at the moment, but they will not be. The most important thing is the shift in human consciousness. The rest will follow easily from that.

*So the inventions can come forth?*

269

All manner of inventions will begin to awaken. And in time you will see that the inventions were just a bridge point between what you thought was possible and what is possible. To the degree that you will at some point outgrow the need of any inventions. We are not suggesting technology has no place, it does indeed mirror what the soul already understands to be absolutely true.

For example, you have your telephones that you wear in your pockets, a hundred years ago that would have been thought impossible. Now it is commonplace. In time you will just be aware that you don't need the telephone. If you want to speak to somebody, you tune into them, their consciousness, you share what you want to share, and it is much quicker. You may share deep insights in the very instantaneousness of a moment and you will both know that this is taking place. The telephone just simply serves as a forerunner to the possibility of insights that you will share instantaneously, if you choose to, with other people.

So all the technology will have developmental stages of great beauty in time to come. But why wait? Dive deep within. Feel that God/Goddess does not expect you to go through some kind of cosmic chart of, this invention - that invention. From A to Z. You can go past the need of technology. You can still use it in the relative state of consciousness that your daily process exists in, but dive deep into the place beyond the need of feeling any separation. Those are the qualities of insight that awaits you. And do function within you now. In varying degrees the conscious mind is already beginning to be aware of this, but there is always more. You can always go a little deeper. And Divinity will walk with you, chuckle with you. Take you down to another level if the trust is there. Never will Divinity force the way. As long as any fear comes up, Divinity steps back and says, "We wait. We wait for the fear to find its own release. And then more will come."

Yes, let us go on with the questionings if you like.

*You said earlier that you are not, in the Spirit world, happy about violence and cruelty. I just wonder if it also means that we, sometime in the future, as human beings stop killing animals.*

Oh, I think that will be easily done. You will easily see that the consciousness you need to awaken to, will no longer resource food from the animals. You will find that your ability to allow more of a direct absorption of energy to sustain and nourish the body. There will probably be for most part of people still needing some sense of food, but you will find that there are resources of energy in the vegetable kingdom, that are little understood today.

A very small part of what we speak of would be revealed through sprouting. If you take the grains or the seeds, the nuts, and you allow them to germinate to varying degrees, the beauty of the energy they carry is unleashed in a magnificent way. And the energies are increased manifold. So that in itself is just a very short illustration of how the ability of the body to absorb energy will be more clearly understood.

And you will refine your taste buds. You will no longer be fooled by modern chemistry that says, "Now, this tastes good, therefore it must be good for you." When in fact quite the opposite might be true when you put into your bodies - now everybody is going to get very nervous - your refined sugars and starches, and your taste delights, such as ice creams and coffees and such. You will not need those when you start to taste the full richness of the food inherent in the plants grown in soil that is rich and alive, and you have not micro waved it, you have not frozen it, you allow it to blossom in the body. And more directly to draw in Divine energy.

Until that time don't beat yourselves up over your diet, but try to notice, "What is the quality of the life force in the food that I ingest in my body?" Without guilt. It is a very important thing. If you get caught in some kind of loop, like the dog chasing its tale, running around and around trying to figure out what God wants you to do, and feeling guilty if you have a bite of a hamburger or something. Perhaps that is more destructive than simply sitting down to a big meal that may have everything on the table, some of which you like and some of which you don't. And the atmosphere is so charged with wonder and joy that the food does not matter. So you could eat meat or not eat meat. If your vibration was clear, you would transform everything. Do you understand?

*Yes. Also thinking about the animals of course.*

Yes. Well, the point being once you start to see where the energy lies, then you would also begin to feel definitely less inclined to eat meat of any form. What perhaps most of all begins to happen for many people, is they realize that the human kingdom and the animal kingdom are closely related. The animals that you share your lives with, that you call pets, you understand in time that they are magnificently aware of their process on the planet. They are generally there to serve as healing instruments. To bring more joy, more spontaneity, more playfulness, more present time reality to the people they share their life experience with.

All of this of course, carries a great emotional baggage from the past. You have arguments, one way or the other, regarding food, regarding what you should eat. Everybody is on some kind of diet. We would like to just simply say, "Where is the life force?" If you grow a plant, perhaps we use the example of a tomato, in your garden and you pick the tomato in the fullness of its ripeness. It has a magnificent flavor. If you go to the grocery store and it is a very commercially developed tomato, it is a wonder it is not square - we tease you a little bit now. But it is picked green. There is not much

272

life force yet available in a green tomato. It has not been ripened. It may be in a sense almost a negative energy in the body. It is picked green. Somehow it is forced into ripeness before it reaches the consumer. But it was never really fully developed in the life force that it carries. That is just one example. And now, don't go out and say, "I can never eat a tomato." Even a green one.

But I would recommend that things that are grown close to you. In the soil that is rich and healthy, relatively close in your own environment. Perhaps with your own activity. There is something that happens in relationship to the earth that you experience that is also a form of nurturance.

Now, in time the energies will be sensed and felt and seen so clearly that people will not be trying to tell others how they aught to do it. Everybody will find the flow that works for them. Before that happens though, simply try to stay away from the heavy indulgence in refined sweetenings. Especially the artificial sweetenings, they are worse than the refined ordinary sweetenings. Try to stay away from high levels of starch and watch the sodium, the salt, do not have a lot of excess salt. Unless you are working a lot physically, and you are perspiring, you are loosing the salt that way, then of course you need to be careful not to loose it.

And then, notice when things are killed in the cooking. You would not eat meat raw, you would cook it. There is a definite value in meat that has not been placed in the microwave. If you are going to have a steak, cook it. Don't put it in the microwave. If you are going to have a cup of pasta, you warm it up with hot water, you mix it, perhaps it is dry, there may still be some life force in it if it is not totally refined. But you warm it up in the microwave. It looks nice, smells nice, tastes nice, nice texture. There is no energy.

273

So, these things are not so complicated. When you start to trust that your body knows before you place the food in the body, how that piece of food is going to affect the body. You can ask in your mind, you can hold your hand over the food, you can do it in different ways, "Does this food enhance my body's awareness? Does it work well in my system?" Perhaps the food is perfectly fine, but you have been having an argument with someone, then the food will not work well in the body. Not because of anything wrong with the food, but because your digestive system is all upset. So these are just simple things. A little prayer, a little meditation, inviting the presence of Spirit, giving thanks for the abundance that you do receive and going on with life. Don't have to be a saint. Do you understand?

*Yes.*

We thank you for the question. It is a very adroit time for that question to come forward. The tricky thing with diet now is that most people are simply eating a lot of junk. So if they bring better food into their body, they are going to have greater clarity of their mind and their soul will come forth with greater wisdom. And then it is a continuing process to continue to refine the dietary function of their particular body. And in that sense everyone is a bit different, each body is unique at any point in time. Perhaps someone has been a vegetarian for fifteen or twenty years and something is going wrong with the body, they may need to eat meat. It may be the best thing they can do for a time. There may be some elements they have been missing. Someone else may have been a meat eater for the past twenty five or thirty years and suddenly they start to realize, "Oh, my gosh, I have to have more vegetables. I have to have more fruits and salads and lettuce and celery and all those things." And they start making juices. And they start loosing the desire for much meat. Someone else may have a Spiritual awakening so profound that they sit down to have a steak, they cannot do it. They sit down to have a piece of chicken, they cannot do it. They finally decide to have a nice piece of very fresh fish, the best you can find, and they simply cannot place it in their body.

Each one is responsible to the awareness that has awakened in them. And in the joy of that, know that Divinity loves you and laughs with you and is not measuring you by your diet. We hope to make that very clear.

We should not hold this instrument too much longer. Perhaps one or two more questionings?

*Does this mean that we will be moving away from mass production of all sorts of food?*

Oh, I think you will find that there will be many things that you function well with, in what you have termed mass production, for basic needs of large numbers of people. But you will take delight in the refinement of individual growth of foods. With joy. With love. The preparation of food with joy and love. And as that extends, you will also find there are many things that you make by hand. Not because they cannot be mass-produced, but because you start to take delight in the artistic accomplishment. For example a purse, now you can sew up a lot of purses in a factory, looking very stylish, the right colors, the right designs etc. But someone comes along and they dream of a design. They sit down. They are working the leather. They are producing the holes. They are stitching. There may be drawing in some bit of painting or dye. And they make a purse that is beautiful and unique and there is a lot of creative, loving energy in it. There will be room for all of that. Do you understand?

*Yes.*

Some things you may find that you highly prize and they are not necessarily very complicated. Life will, in a way, simplify. You will not need the vast amounts of stuff that you surround yourselves with. Everybody got nervous, didn't they? We are teasing you a little bit now.

When you go camping, when you go out into the wilderness, you don't want to carry a lot of stuff with you. You want to enjoy the nature. And we are speaking now of that simplification of lightening the load. You may find that there is a time where you share the abundance with others. Maybe you have things in common with a few friends. For example, maybe you have a desire to go boating. And four or five of you say, "Well, let us own a boat *together*, so that we don't have to have a huge expense." And not having enough time to enjoy the boat as often as you wish, it is still available to you. And shared with others, in a way, may make that a more wonderful experience than just having it sit in a store room for the next five years. Do you understand?

*Yes.*

Some of these examples may not serve, but I think you get the point. It is a simplification of the energies you expand in daily life, so you have the room to express creatively the things you want to do.

And more and more you will find the development of insight such that you want to share it, particularly with the children. You will begin to see that these old souls in young bodies, are calling out to you to share with them whatever it is you can give them to allow them to wake up more quickly. So the poems, the drawings, the art patterns, the teachings, the classes, the books, whatever, become a kind of joyous expression of the soul to help enhance, through teaching, the wisdom of the children that are being born. So they may more quickly help this shift in consciousness across the planet that we are speaking of.

I don't think we should hold the body longer. It is our great joy to share with you.

# Meditation

*If you would take just a moment*
*to sit in quietude.*

*Just be aware that around you now,*
*there are those many in Spirit*
*who join with you as well*
*in this time of meditative energy.*

*And feel the deep link to the planet*
*as though your soul sits astride the earth.*
*Somehow in the mind,*
*see you sitting on the planet.*

*And the earth and the heaven*
*in deep communion*
*through your being.*

*Just feel that energy.*

[Silence]

*It has been our great joy to share with you.*
*Know that you walk always in the light.*

*And as your courage deepens*
*to embrace that light more directly,*
*so too then will the joy of life expand.*

*It has been our joy to share.*
*God bless you.*

278

# About Lin David Martin

The hunger for Divine contact has been strong in me since I was a young child. I was not consciously able to expressing it then, but I always had this sense of something more. I remember one time as a kid I was lying in the grass on a blanket with my family, looking at the stars and thinking a little bit about the immensity of the Universe. That moment was significant somehow. I have thought back to that many times because it touched something reliable and deep. Like the hunger to know more. The sense that it would be impossible to be alone. *That the Universe has got to be filled with life.*

I had a sense that somehow I was here by choice. That there was a rime and a reason to being present in the body. I did not think in those terms then, although I do remember as a six or seven years old or so, looking at my parents thinking, "I picked some good parents this time." Being a little shocked there and then, but at the same time feeling this old me in a young body. I never spoke about this.

I did not grow up in a household that was particularly religious externally. My mother tended towards a religious orientation, my father did not, and I did not feel that either one of them were right or wrong. It was not a contest in any sense. There was this substance to the inner worth of the individual, that was present. My parents respected each other. I never saw them argue or fight.

My mindset would probably have been considered, if I look back on it now, somewhat atheistic or agnostic. In the sense that I was not thinking of a God in the Heavens. I was feeling more of an alignment to a Universal Consciousness. When I encountered religious teachings or thoughts that were common in the culture, I did not disregard them, but I felt that people did not know what they were talking about. Even though there was something behind their expression that was very true, the social form of evangelical Christianity was often a cover up for people's anxieties. Especially in their desire to convert somebody.

I had this subtle sense that life had meaning, and there was actually some kind of Divine Law activated by people's thoughts and experiences. But it certainly was not a judgmental God. It was not a harsh dictatorial view of God, which was all too often the kind of thoughts that people had about religion. There was a lot of fear-based thinking then, and I just had a sense that that could not be the way the Universe functions. Now I can put words on it. Then I could not have expressed it. I had just a kind of an inner knowingness.

I got involved with my spiritual search as a teenager. One time I went with my mother to a Quaker meeting. There was a lot of spirit energy present. I was impressed, but as a young man I was not attracted to a group of only older people. I wanted something with a little cultural context that I was involved with at the time. I searched out different metaphysically oriented groups in Phoenix (my home town) for about a year, but I did not find what I was looking for yet.

I had some rather powerful experiences of spiritual awakening, a quickening of energy, at the age of about seventeen. As a preliminary to that, I had my first experience with a psychic. A close friend's girlfriend, now wife, had been seeing a psychic. It developed that my friend and his brother were going to this psychic also, and I just came along. I was not there for a reading. We went in and sat in her living room, the three of us, and she came and called me in first. I had no clue what this was about. I sat down opposite her in a chair, in this little room, and she closed her eyes and started telling me about my life, the people in it, and what was going on in their consciousness. I was dumb founded. It was so accurate and so true. I had no doubt in my mind about the reading's accuracy, its validity, the truth of it was absolutely clear to me. She helped confirm that there is another part of the mind that can function.

I realized that my neat little picture of the Universe, which was perhaps broader than how most of my friends pictured the Universe, was still way too small. Before that session I had always had a great sense that the mind has incredible potential. There was never a doubt in my thoughts that the mind, when it was fully understood, would hold amazing keys to development and insights and tremendous resources that we all can draw upon.

In the following three days, after this psychic reading, I thought about what she had done. My basic question was, *"How did she do it?"*

Shortly after, I was driving down the freeway when I suddenly went into three different people's mind with my own mind. I saw their consciousness from the inside. Back then, in the late fifties, we did not talk about these things, but I felt I could approach and ask two of them about it. Both of them verified that my perception was accurate. This settled in my mind how the psychic lady had done what she did. I realized that *minds can connect.* We are not just separate islands; we are connected underneath the surface.

Within a couple of weeks following, there was a book on my parent's coffee table. The title of the book was "There is a River," by Thomas Sugrue. It was the story of trance channel Edgar Cayce. The timing was perfect for this book to show up in my life. I had read a case study earlier by Hypnotist Morey Bernstein called "The search for Bridey Murphy." That book touched upon the possibility for reincarnation and it had that ring of authenticity about it. At this point, in a part of my mind, I considered reincarnation a possibility and I knew that minds can connect. I was ready to go deeper.

I delved into "There is a River." I took it all in. The story amazed me, and I had to read the latter part over and over again. It summarizes the philosophy that came through Edgar Cayce in the latter part of his life, were people started to ask more metaphysical questions, not just questions regarding medical problems. It was at that point that the whole process of reincarnation opened in Cayce's work. The great synopsis or overview presented is like a synthesis of both eastern and western thinking. It still is amazing in the way it could incorporate these seemingly opposite views. I remember reading that chapter thinking, "This is really difficult stuff, but very direct." It took me a while to assimilate it.

I read all the Edgar Cayce material I could find. Three books of strong significance were Dr. Gina Cerminara's books: "Many Mansions," "World Within," and "Many Lives, Many Loves." All based on the Cayce material regarding reincarnation. Then I came across Paramahansa Yoganada's autobiography: "Autobiography of a Yogi." That was probably the most important book I have ever read. Another book I liked a lot was Carl Jung's autobiography: "Memories, Dreams and Reflections." It also touched a cord in me.

Overall, this was in a three years period. I was taking night classes, working my way through college. A good friend of mine, from my mathematics class back then, suddenly had this experience of speaking in tongues in the middle of a church choir. I was the one studying metaphysics and she was more involved with ordinary church things. She explained it was like a bolt of light went through her. A very powerful experience obviously. I recognized from my studies that it was a valid religious experience and part of me was going, "Darn, here I am studying all this stuff and she is having the experience." I had been meditating for a while in my own devotional way, inspired by Yogananda's autobiography. Strong energies were happening, but no speaking in tongues. My classmate's experience tweaked my curiosity, so I started going to some of the prayer meetings she was going to. I took my sister with me one time and she had the experience of speaking in tongues. I took another friend with me and he had the experience. I did not have it and I kept wondering what was wrong with me.

Then, one evening when I walked into the room where the prayer meeting was held, I felt like I was walking into a river of energy - about knee high. The energy was so strong I could not stand up. So here I was on the floor, the young Methodist minister came over and started prophesying over me. Most of what he said I don't remember anymore, but at the time he said, "You are going to be a Spiritual Teacher." Something inside of me went, "This is true." I did not know what it meant and I had no idea what would evolve from it.

Going to those meetings was very good. But I had a feeling, which I understand now, that there was a lot of spirits in the room. And my feeling was that they had so much more they could give people, but the context of the group thinking was that it had to be very biblical. I knew that spirits were real, because I knew reincarnation was true. I had a feeling that these spirit teachers present would have liked to give more in that context, but it was not right for the people to think in those terms. I could feel that the quality and the energy were great, but the restriction on what could be taught was quite strong. People were still struggling with the fear of "back sliding" or the fear of the devil. They were still dealing with the typical Christian image of heaven and hell.

That night, after this profound experience, going home I felt like somebody had plugged me into 220 volts. My body was just this river of energy. I woke up in the middle of the night, and for some reason I felt I had to talk to my brother that I was sharing a bedroom with. He was across the room, asleep in bed. I tried to talk to him, but I could not speak English. *I was speaking in tongues.* I was finally having this experience and for the next three days I went around with this river of energy flowing through me. After that it gradually dissipated. In classic terms you could say I had experienced an awakening of the Kundalini.

One of the effects from this experience was that my sensitivity opened in new ways. If I was going to eat something, and I got it almost in my mouth – like an intention to eat it – I would feel in that moment how the food was going to affect my body. I did not want to believe that, because it was clearly steering me away from junk food. I had not researched it, I had not thought it through. I remember a payday candy-bar, which had a core of candy and then dipped in nuts. Sweet and salty and crunchy. In my personality mind I concluded that this had to be relatively healthy. "Sugar is just energy," like the sugar companies wants you to believe, and peanuts are good for you. So I would go to put that in my mouth and I would feel this incredible tiredness come over me. I would think, "It cannot do that to me. I am stronger than that." So I would eat the candy-bar, and half an hour later this incredible tiredness would come over me. I thought I could control my body's reaction with my mind, but my intuition would show me exactly how that food was going to affect my body.

Because of this I started changing my diet. Which was as important as anything else in my overall growth. In reading more of the Cayce material I found out that, in its own subtle way, the Cayce readings for spiritual growth were geared toward eating more healthy food. It is part of the process. A change of diet can be as singularly important as any other thing in a spiritual search.

Until now I had been reading and studying a lot, but had not found my spiritual home yet. A friend across the street was getting ordained in this new age church. I was invited to go. I went together with a couple of others to this little church in south Phoenix. The church was filled to overflowing. There was stand up room only. The guest speaker of that day was Dr. Gina Cerminara. I was impressed by the fact that she was there.

Then this man got up and did a demonstration of "blind-fold billet" or clairvoyance. They passed out pieces of paper and people wrote questions on them. As they were collecting the papers with the questions, this man on the podium was getting absolutely completely blindfolded. He took the pieces of paper, held them one by one up against his forehead and gave clairvoyant messages to individuals present. The energy went sky-high. The room felt electric. The third person he came to was me. When that happened, I felt this bolt of energy go through me. It was the same energy that had happened at the prayer meeting.

*I knew I had just found my Spiritual home.* And it became that, for the next fourteen years.

I ended up going to classes and studying at this new age center/church: The University of Life. Dr. Richard Ireland, the founder, was incredibly talented on every level. You name it and he could do it: X-ray clairvoyance, physical phenomena, medium-ship, wonderful teachings, out of the body experiences etc. All of that was just part and parcel of his experience. It was easy for him to help at whatever level of experience people were having.

After four years of ministerial training, I became a minister. The University of Life was the main thrust in my life for quite a while. I went through college. I got my first four-year degree and took a lot of extra classes in religious studies, which at that time were not part of the University. They were offered as optional extra credit courses – lightly attached to the University. Later when I went back to do graduate work, a lot of those classes I had been taking earlier, had been shifted into the humanities department. So I took some more classes during my graduate years.

My graduate studies centered around the metaphysical and psychic interests of the noted philosopher and psychologist William James. I wrote a master thesis on him. One book of his of great interest was "Varieties of Religious Experience." He was published in the early part of the 1900. His work is still relevant today. Historically William James was a pioneer in parapsychology, working with both the British and American Society for Psychical Research.

Rabbi Plotkin was my favorite teacher in religious studies. He was quite gifted in his insight into the Old Testament. And he understood psychic phenomena very well. When he was a young man, going to rabbinical school, he had been invited by three other Rabbis, which is the tradition, to study the Kabala with them. You could not go out to find a place to study it, you had to get invited. So here he is in my graduate years, teaching a class of three or four hundred students on the Kabala. I was happy to be part of that.

This was my external academic environment at that time, but the more important process was going on with the church. In my early engagement with the University of Life, I gave public talks. At one point something shifted in how I was going about it. Where I before had prepared my talks, suddenly the preparation got in the way. A new teaching process developed. Just before the lecture, I would meditate on an idea or a theme. While being in front of the class, this extremely beautifully organized lecture would come through me. I could not have prepared something like it in my ordinary mind. In a sense I got inspired. It just opened the floodgates of my soul.

At University of Life we would have healing work available before the main service. Somebody would get up, give a talk and lead a meditation. At the same time there was a dedicated healing room where people could come and receive healing for two or three minutes each. It was very effective. My healing ability had opened up already back when I had the Pentecostal experience, and I was comfortable with it. But the healing was the extent of my psychic exposure. I did not want to be a psychic. Healing was okay. I felt fine about that. Teaching was okay. But there were a lot of good psychics at the church and I did not think they needed another one. My resistance was huge about that. The main resistance was to the thought of somebody taking guidance from me - the Spirit working through me. I had great faith in Spirit, but I did not have great faith in their ability to work through me in that way.

I was going to weekly classes with Crowfoot, the Spirit teacher through Richard Ireland. The Spirit taught trance class sessions. Those classes were quite incredible. The space that would happen during a class would be like I was home. I would come out of that class, feeling like Crowfoot had talked directly to my heart. And twenty-five other people would walk out feeling the same way. The compassion was so strong.

This is the thing about the American-Indian tradition; people will often read books that are written maybe by an anthropologist that will include a lot of the cultural traditional forms, but this class was not that way at all. It was a very spiritual homogenized energy. We were aware that there were other Spirit Teachers present, and Crowfoot said that he was also being a channel for other Spirit Teachers at the same time. The sense was very Universal. Of truth being taught and spoken directly to your inner consciousness, not just the outer mind. The approach was very simple. There was a lot of patience and compassion. It was not extremely mystical or esoteric. It felt very real, very solid, very grounded. As a teacher, Crowfoot did not have room for spiritual "space cases." He kept you grounded in the physical plane with a spiritual consciousness opening.

Crowfoot's teaching was never directed toward developing a lot of psychics. It was focused on helping people wake up spiritually and he said the rest would follow from that. I was in this class for eight years.

There was a point where I started having a lot of out of the body experiences. Lot of the times they would be verified. There were people in the organization that I would have an out of the body experience with, and they would remember. When we met after it happened, we would talk about it. That helped me understand the difference between a vivid dream and an actual out of the body experience.

Somewhere in that process I was getting very intuitive, very psychic. I would often know things about other people's lives long before they would happen. There were times when I would have these predictive dreams about the whole next day in detail. Sometimes I would have dreams about things happening months later. They all did happen. I did not say anything to anybody. I did not want anybody to think of me as a psychic. I was testing it out in a way, for my own skeptical self's sake.

The trance work took about ten years to fully blossom. I had been sitting in trance classes all those years, so I understood the energy around trance as much as you can understand it without doing it. And doing it was probably for me the missing piece. I look back and realize that I could have been doing trance work much sooner. I was teaching a children's class for a while. The teaching process was highly inspired, and looking back at it, I was teaching half in

290

trance already. It was a good experience. My meditation state had also been deep enough for years, but my personality had somehow convinced itself that healing was okay, psychic work was not. I had them in divided categories.

Then this profound out of the body experience happened, where I was in a room with about fifty people in a big circle. I was walking around, stopping in front of each individual, giving private messages. It was very real, and is still very real. I even remember some of the messages, which I normally don't do. I realized the messages did not come from me. I was in a light trance, a conscious trance. I was aware of the Spirit teacher working through me and also of the amazing compassion that was flowing. While in the experience I was thinking, "Oh, this is what it is to be in the channeling state. And it is the same energy that is happening in healing." So finally I made a linkage between the two. Reflecting on this, I thought, "If this is the same energy as healing, and I have already said yes to healing, I cannot say no to this light channeling state or clairvoyant state."

One or two weeks later, I mentioned my out of the body experience to a friend who was a trance channel and he said, "Oh yes, I remember that. I was there. The next time I am on the podium, I am going to call you up and you are going to give messages." So he did. I got up and gave three messages. Beforehand I had no clue to what I would be saying, but I just went back into that place where that same kind of energy was happening. It was not as strong in the physical body as it was in that out of the body state, which is often typical. Out of the body can feel stronger. But the messages were accurate and the ice was broken. I sat down afterwards and was a bit shaky. It was a scary experience for my ego, but I realized it was good and accurate. For the next year I gave individual messages in groups, once or twice a week, in that clairvoyance state. My feeling was that, over time, the channeling got closer to the quality of that first time, out of the body. It continued to develop.

A small group of friends would get together to practice a bit. We would meditate first and then we would do "billets." (French for a piece of paper.) We would write down questions on a piece of paper, fold them up, and on the outside we would put a symbol or a number. We would maybe throw in a couple of questions each in a basket. Then we would take turns in picking one and giving a psychic impression. It was a way for us to work in a small group and bypassing our egos, not knowing what the question was and whom it belonged to. It was great practice and we all got very good at it. We met for a couple of years to practice.

One evening I was doing a group clairvoyance with "billets," about one year after the initial conscious channeling state opened up, I started to feel the same Spirit teacher overshadowing my consciousness. I lost the awareness of the room and became aware that he was speaking. I did not know what he was saying. I was in this immense state of ecstasy. I remember thinking, "Okay, this is trance. If it is ecstatic, I am all for trance." A couple more people came into the room while I was in trance and I was totally unaware of it. When I came out of the trance state, I knew what had happened, but I did not know what I had said. When the trance finally opened in me, it was almost fully developed from the very start because I had been sitting in trance classes and been around it for so long,

The first two or three months of doing trance work, I would sometimes do sessions for a small family group. It happened that I was in trance for two or three hours. I think they were cleaning out the channel, getting that spiritual opening really opened and establishing the connection.

In the meantime I had been teaching a parapsychology class for adults at The University of Life. I would go to teach the class, but I would start to lose focus. I was half in trance already. So I finally said, "Well, I know what they want me to do. We are not going to have any more parapsychology class. We are going to have a trance class." So we moved the whole class into the designated trance room. I became a channel for a weekly trance class with this ongoing study group. That went on for about a year. It was very helpful to me. I also started to get requests to do trance classes for smaller groups in people's homes, outside the center. That was my first step on my own, away from my spiritual home.

Almost fourteen years after I joined The University of Life, Spirit one day popped into my mind and said, "It is time to go. You have got to leave." It took about two till three months to get uprooted from my spiritual home. It was like leaving the nest.

I started getting invitations to teach in California, Oregon, Washington, New York, New Jersey and southeast Canada. So I was traveling. It was such an expansion. Such a feeling of freedom. There were two one-day workshops that developed from all the work I had done and been a part of at The University of Life. One was on healing and the other on intuition. The form changed from shorter classes to longer one-day workshops. Then I combined them into a weekend. The workshop format continued to unfold itself. Later on I got invited to Europe, first in Sweden, then Norway, Denmark, Germany, France, Italy and Greece. That was when the long-term workshops/trainings opened up. Soon I was traveling five or six months out of a year doing workshops and classes in Europe.

Much of my work has been, and still is, to help people open up to their own psychic abilities. Always centered in the Heart. Since I developed slowly and over time myself, and had to work through quite a bit of resistance, I understand quite well the nuances of all the little steps along the way. Spirit has always guided me in these processes. In the past if I planned something for the group that Spirit did not think they were ready for, he would pop into my mind and telling me what else to do. So you could say Spirit has largely formed my work, and still is.

The reality, I think, is that we all seek God/Goddess. Consciously or unconsciously, that is still what we are seeking for. And we may go about it and find it in all the wrong ways, as people often do. Trying to put substance to it, saying it must be this or it must be that. But it is the light, the energy, and the consciousness hiding *behind* the physical substance, that we are truly surrounded with.

I think the deepest joy comes from our longing for God, and when we touch upon the process in a way that is experiential, we feel something of the Divine Presence. Then that feels to be the most essential part of the process. And we can always have a longing for more.


*Private Sessions available in*
*Trance Channeling, Clairvoyance,*
*Healing and Spiritual Mentoring.*
(In person or by phone)

*In addition, Lin offers workshops and classes*
*in the US and Europe.*

Contact Lin David Martin at:
Home/Office:           (1) 928-634-1345
Cell phone:            (1) 928-274-1911
Email:                 lindavidmartin@yahoo.com
Web site:              www.lindavidmartin.com

# Trances Where and When

297

# Points of Insight & Notes to Myself

*We know it is not a normal practice*
*to write in this type of book,*
*but sometimes Inspiration strikes*
*while reading or pursuing meditation.*

*Please use these pages for your very own*
*expressions in the joy of awakening.*

Namaste

# Points of Insight & Notes to Myself

# Points of Insight & Notes to Myself

# Points of Insight & Notes to Myself

# Points of Insight & Notes to Myself

# Points of Insight & Notes to Myself

# Points of Insight & Notes to Myself

# Points of Insight & Notes to Myself

# Points of Insight & Notes to Myself

CPSIA information can be obtained at www.ICGtesting.com
Printed in the USA
LVOW040304230212

270025LV00002B/53/A

9 780976 435204